Does Your Resume Wear Blue Jeans?

The Student's First Guide to Finding a Real Job After College

C. Edward Good

William G. Fitzpatrick

Prima Publishing
P.O. Box 1260BK
Rocklin, CA 95677
(916) 786-0426

Production by Melanie Field and Jennifer Boynton, Bookman Productions
Copyediting by James Nageotte
Interior design by Suzanne Montazer
Typography by Bookends Typesetting
Cover design by The Dunlavey Studio

Library of Congress Cataloging-in-Publication Data

Good, C. Edward.
    Does your resume wear blue jeans? : the student's first guide to finding a real job / C. Edward Good.
      p. cm.
    Originally published: Charlottesville, VA: Word Store, © 1985 (1988 printing)
    ISBN 1-55958-293-6 (pbk.) : $9.95
    1. Resumes (Employment) 2. College students—Employment.
I. Title.
HF5383.G5623 1993
650.14—dc20   92-41616
                                              CIP

93 94 95 96 RRD 10 9 8 7 6 5 4 3 2 1

Printed in the United States of America

How to Order:

Quantity discounts are available from the publisher, Prima Publishing, P.O. Box 1260BK, Rocklin, CA 95677; telephone: (916) 786-0426. On your letterhead include information concerning the intended use of the books and the number of books you wish to purchase.

Contents

Preface   vii
Acknowledgments   x
Introduction   xi

CHAPTER 1 Let Me Be Subtle: You're for Sale   1
Realities of the Job Search

A-Marketing You Will Go   2
Your Competitive Edge   3
What "They" Want   3
Trustworthy, Loyal, Helpful . . .   5
Honesty and Speed: Attributes for the 1990s   19
Friendly, Courteous, Kind . . .   21

CHAPTER 2 Of Resumes That Wear Blue Jeans   23
Keys to Successful Self-Marketing

Restyling Your Self-Presentation   25
Take a Deep Breath . . .   30
Go Blow Your Horn   31
Money, Location, Job   35
Ask Yourself Some Questions   37
You've Only Just Begun   38

CHAPTER 3 Thirty Seconds of Air Time   *39*
The Importance of Your Resume

Why Do I Need a Resume?   40
The Definition of a Resume   40
A Thirty-Second Toothpaste Commercial   41
Thirty-Second Scan Rule   43
Meet the Employment Manager   44
Improving Your Odds   46
Getting to Know Your Consumer   47
How to Produce a Resume: Two Choices   48
The Perfect Resume   50
Types of Resumes   51
Which Resume Is Right for You?   58
Resume Structure   59

CHAPTER 4 What Goes Where   *71*
Inside Your Resume

Overview   72
Visiting the Various Headings   72
Sequencing Information   103
Creating Leads   106
Problems with Dates   109

CHAPTER 5 Write This Way, Folks!   *113*
Rules for Grammar and Style

Resume Talk: Listings   113
Resume Talk: Sentences   114
Grammatical Mistakes   115
Matters of Style   119
So Much for Content and Style   122

CHAPTER 6 Balloons and Dancing Bears   *123*
Resume Formatting

First Impressions: Sizing People Up   123
First Impressions: Sizing Up Your Resume   124
The Importance of Formatting   124
The Graphics of Positioning   126
The Graphics of Emphasis   136

Graphic Mistakes 139
Formatting Summary 142

CHAPTER 7 A Firm Handshake 145
  Resume Production

Three Production Decisions 145
Professional Resume Services 151

CHAPTER 8 Who Is Justinius Regal? 153
  Sample Resume Formats

Copying Resumes Is Hazardous to Your Career 153
Copying Formats Is Not So Hazardous 155

CHAPTER 9 How to Dig for Paydirt 165
  Prospecting

Surveying Your Market 165
Where to Start: The Library 166
Essentials of Prospecting 172
Drumming Up Interviews 172
Drumming Up Leads 173
Transmittal Letters 176
Supplies and Production 189
The All-Important Follow-Up 190
Prospecting in Numbers 191

CHAPTER 10 Help! 193
  And Where to Find It

Agencies 194
College Placement Office (Even If You're
  No Longer a Student) 198
A Book, a Mirror—How About a Candle? 209

CHAPTER 11 Your Product Demonstration 211
  The Interview

Clothes 212
Advance Work 214
Your Grand Debut 217

CHAPTER 12 You Want *How* Much?   223
    Salary Negotiation

Knowing What You're Worth   223
The Power of the Purse   224
Benefits   226
Other Compensation   228
Knowledge Is Power   229

CHAPTER 13 P.S.   231
    Your Job

Appendix   233
Index   237
About the Authors   243

Preface

AHHHH. YOU FINALLY PICKED me off the shelf and opened me up. That feels good. Kinda like stretching after a nap. Keep it up. Flip over a few pages. I need the exercise.

Congratulations. You picked the right one, the Blue Jeans book, as I'm called by people in the know. I was originally written by Ed Good in 1985 and published by his publishing company, LEL Enterprises. Now I've been rewritten by Ed Good and Bill Fitzpatrick, expanded quite a bit, and republished by Prima Publishing.

Ed and Bill, my authors, joined forces and wrote me, *Does Your Resume Wear Blue Jeans?*, and my good friend sitting there on the shelf next to me, *Does Your Resume Wear Combat Boots?* Ed used to be a law professor but made a rather dramatic career change when he resigned from his cushy job at the University of Virginia and started his own business, Word Store, a word-processing and copy-center business in Charlottesville, Virginia. At Word Store, Ed developed the Legal Employment Letter Service and resume services to help job seekers find employment throughout the country. Over the years, he wrote resumes for hundreds of job seekers, all kinds of people, from a cook at the county jail to the vice president of a Fortune 500 company.

Recently Ed sold Word Store to Lisa Miller, a former Word Store employee and a graduate of the University of Virginia. Now Ed heads LEL Enterprises, a company providing on-site training in effective writing for law firms and federal agencies. He also conducts career transition seminars for the United States Secret Service and the Department of Justice.

Bill, my other author, is a retired Command Sergeant Major who consults with the Non Commissioned Officers Association. Bill travels all over the world giving career transition seminars to members of our armed services. He has helped thousands of service personnel prepare resumes and job-search campaigns to find top positions in the private sector following their military careers.

When Ed and Bill originally got together, they took the old Blue Jeans book and combined it with lots of Bill's ideas to produce the Combat Boots book. Now they've expanded both books.

You've made an excellent choice in books for several reasons. First, most of those other job-search books are rather stuffy. They get way too fancy and high falutin'. I, on the other hand, like to liven things up. After all, the job-search process can be rather stressful, so I hope you find my light-hearted approach eases the burden a bit.

Second, you'll find that my advice is practical and down to earth. The way I figure it, there are only three ways you can get a job: (1) call somebody on the phone and ask, (2) meet somebody in person and ask, and (3) write somebody a letter and ask. Let's face it, you're not likely to find a whole slew of eager employers knocking on your front door and pleading for you to report to work on Monday. I also figure that the more people you ask, the greater your chances of success. So you'll find within my pages some no-nonsense advice on how to launch a self-marketing campaign. As you'll see, it's a numbers game. And it's fun to play.

Third, I'm a much more mature book than the old Blue Jeans book. I've expanded my horizons to include the entire job search: deciding what you want to do, writing your resume, drumming up interviews, succeeding in the interview, and negotiating for a good salary.

So you've made the right choice. Now go on over to the cashier. You'll find the cost is a small price to pay for top-notch advice. Then take me home and begin to read. Follow my advice. Launch your job-search campaign. And soon success will come your way.

Acknowledgments

MANY THANKS TO WILLIAM VANDOREN of Charlottesville, Virginia, who took our manuscript, scrutinized every sentence, made his mark when needed, and polished our prose into the finished and publishable product.

We express our appreciation to Mrs. Karen Knierim of the University of Virginia Office of Career Planning and Placement, whose insights and experience enabled us to include an insider's view of the many services that career-planning professionals provide in today's colleges and universities.

Our appreciation also goes to Bert Davis, owner of the Bert Davis Agency in New York City, for his observations into the workings of a metropolitan employment agency.

Introduction

OUR BOOK JUST HAD to get in a few words by itself. It wanted to take over the entire manuscript, but we had to draw the line somewhere. So it came up with that clever little Preface; we take the responsibility for the rest.

We hope you'll profit from the approach to job searching you find in *Does Your Resume Wear Blue Jeans?* and the companion volume for military people, *Does Your Resume Wear Combat Boots?* We've tried to demystify the job-searching process and bring it down to earth. Our approach is not all that complicated, once you get the hang of it. It's based on some rather simple principles: first, you must not sell yourself short; second, you're your own best salesperson; third, you must at all times maintain an upbeat, positive attitude; fourth, you must recognize the job search as a game; and fifth, you must play that game by some widely recognized rules.

Overriding all these principles, however, is one universal truth in any job search: the more you ask, the more you get. The more people you approach and ask for employment, the more you'll get rejected. The more people you approach and ask for employment, the more interviews you'll get. The more want ads you respond to, the more rejection letters you'll get. The more want ads you respond to, the more interviews you'll get. The more headhunters you write to, the more headhunters who'll turn you down. The more headhunters you write to, the more headhunters who'll take you on. The more letters you send out, the more rejections you'll receive. The more letters you send out, the more interviews you'll land. The more phone calls you make, the more bad news you'll hear. The more phone calls you make, the more good news will come your way.

Get the picture? It's a numbers game. A game you win by increasing the numbers.

You'll find these principles permeating our approach to the job search. We believe first-class resumes accompanying first-class cover letters always get results. We believe those people who exude confidence in their correspondence with future employers always win in the end. We believe people who insist on excellence in their approach to the job search and in their performance of their jobs are the people who ultimately get ahead in this world.

We've tried to illustrate how these principles work in real-world situations. Many of these situations we've jointly shared, so we'll speak in the book using the first-person plural (we, our, etc.). In some situations, however, anecdotes belong uniquely to one author and not the other. In the Blue Jeans book, you'll sometimes encounter an "I" or a "me" or a "my." When you do, the "I" is author Ed Good. In the Combat Boots book, the "I" is author Bill Fitzpatrick. We hope these pronominal shifts won't confuse.

So flip some more pages. Consider our advice. Apply our principles to your own job search. The results are guaranteed. You'll get interviews and ultimately a job.

CHAPTER 1

Let Me Be Subtle: You're for Sale

Realities of the Job Search

FOR THE FIRST TIME—or, perhaps, for the tenth time—you're looking for a job. It might be an entry-level job, a highly skilled technical position, a critical step in a career in top management. You might be looking because you need to develop in your profession, because you want to shift careers, because you could be laid off in a corporate cutback, or because you're just starting out in the world of employment. Whatever the situation, the job search is always a time to do some serious thinking about the future—to determine what you want from employment and what you have to offer a company or other organization.

The time for thinking and deciding about your job search ideally begins long before the search itself. But whether you're launching your search today or next month, the process will benefit from a heavy dose of reality, beginning with this crude but essential analogy: You are a product that is for sale. You have skills, you are willing to provide services, and you expect to be paid for those services. Your future employer is buying the product—your skills and your services.

As you probably know, however, employers aren't in business to do you a favor, or to recognize and reward your qualities and skills. No business opens its doors in America unless it plans to make a profit. Even nonprofit corporations and organizations must make a "profit" to stay in business. Somebody has to pay the wages and expenses. A company can't keep operating without some sort of income potential. That may sound cold and harsh, but, in America, it's not only okay but quite necessary to make a buck. So you'd better understand the basic rule of all employment: If you're not part of the profit picture, you won't be part of the picture for long.

A-Marketing You Will Go

Now that you know that you're for sale, how do you go out there and sell yourself effectively? The best way is to see yourself as a product and then adjust all of your job-search efforts to make sure potential employers understand how they can make money from hiring you. To do that, you have to understand some basic marketing strategy.

In sales, there is a rule that states, "Don't sell the features, sell the benefits." Features and benefits provide the basis of all sales. People don't buy a product simply because it's attractive (features), they buy the product for what they will get out of it (benefits). For example, you won't buy a Caribbean cruise because the ship is of Norwegian registry with titanium-plated twin screw propellers and watertight compartments, has a world-class buffet, and makes port calls in Martinique and Barbados as well as Aruba. Those features help make what you're buying possible. But what you're buying is the fun and relaxation of a cruise, a much-needed break, a honeymoon, or an escape from reality. You don't buy a sports car because it has a T-Top roof, 800 horsepower, CD player with twenty-seven speakers, and a bright red paint job. What you really buy is the ability to sit at a stoplight and pick up girls (or guys). People don't buy a candy bar because it has an attractive wrapper, a creamy caramel center, or nuts and chocolate. They buy because of the satisfaction they get from eating the candy bar.

You, as a job seeker, have certain features that will make you attractive to a potential employer. Your job is to find out what those features are, and then have a plan to show potential employers how they will benefit from hiring you.

Your Competitive Edge

Your features alone won't do the job. Those job offers everyone at some time or another dreams about receiving simply because of how talented, experienced, wonderful, or personable they are never seem to materialize. You must translate your qualities into benefits employers can understand, and then communicate them to the people who will be interested. In short, you must determine your competitive edge.

Everybody has one. You must be confident you can succeed because you have the assets that will help you to achieve your goals. Determining your competitive edge is an important part of preparing for your job search. Although we may paint a bleak picture about what you can't sell, we are very strong on what you can sell—assuming that, in addition to skills, you offer the kinds of traits employers look for.

What "They" Want

Most people haven't the foggiest idea what employers are looking for. Even if they have some insight into employers' desires, they rarely make the connection that all the elements of their job search should try to respond to those wants. Sure, most people think quite correctly that their resumes and cover letters should impress the employer. But they incorrectly try to do that by listing the events of their lives, rather than by portraying their experiences as evidence of the attributes employers want.

You won't find a good ad agency developing an expensive ad campaign without first trying to find out what the consumer wants. Yes, some ads try to impose new likes and dislikes on the consumer. But most of the successful ones cater to known consumer desires.

As we'll explain in a later chapter, you'll have about thirty seconds of the employment manager's time to make your pitch. But what pitch? It makes a great deal of sense to know exactly what the employer is looking for. Especially in those precious few seconds when the employment manager picks up your resume for that first, quick review.

The best way to find out what employers want is to ask them. That's exactly what the College Placement Council did when it surveyed the top college recruiters. Even if you're not planning to try to crack into a Fortune 500 company, many career counselors would agree that this list pretty much describes the desires of employers, public and private, large and small. We do know that, as employers ourselves, we want employees with attributes like the sixteen cited in the College Placement Council survey.

Here, then, is your marketing survey. Here's what your future employer hopes you will be. As you read our description of these ideal attributes, consider how your background and experience demonstrate the qualities employers want in their employees. If you're a professional or businessperson, relate these qualities primarily to your work experience, your development within your profession, your climb up the ladder, your goals, your accomplishments, your education (whether recent or way back in the mists of time), and your community service. If you're a graduating college student, think about your summer jobs, your college activities, your writing experience, your travel, your internships, your athletics, your music, your volunteer work, and, of course (you were hoping we'd leave these out?), your grades. If you're a homemaker reentering the workforce after raising your family, think primarily about your experience in parenting, in serving the community, in working part-time, in raising money for charities, in working with focus groups, or in attending continuing education programs. If you're a graduating high school student, think about your activities, your academics, your sports, your music, your church, your community work, and your employment mowing yards or sitting babies.

Whatever your background, think of those experiences in your life that show how you have exactly what the employer wants. You'll then begin to see the shape, direction, and strategy of your self-marketing plan, from beginning to end, from resume to interview to salary negotiation to that first day on the job.

Trustworthy, Loyal, Helpful . . .

Here are the sixteen attributes most frequently mentioned by the nation's top corporate recruiters. Just listen to what your consumer wants.

1. Ability to Communicate

To be of much value to an employer you've got to be able to communicate. Beyond requiring a certain primitive level of work, they want you to be able to organize your thoughts and present them coherently through the written or spoken word. Employers recognize that the brainiest candidate for a position is not very valuable if he or she can't share thoughts and ideas with others. They know how much time and money are wasted by convoluted research studies that wind up gathering dust on a shelf. They know the loss of productivity occasioned by the meeting that stretches on forever because the participants can't speak to the point.

Employers also recognize communication as a two-way street. They want someone who not only can write and speak but also listen. They want someone who can listen to an assignment, follow instructions, ask questions, clarify ambiguities, and finish the task in good time.

Finally, employers know the importance of "vibes." At least, the good ones do. (I say this because, of course, and as every experienced employee knows, once in a while an employer will have rather lousy "vibes," and you need to evaluate these as well as be aware of your own, during the job-search process.) Employers want someone with the right presence, with the right body language—someone who commands the respect of other employees. Employers do not want to hire someone who comes into a room and gives off the feeling that someone just left.

Can you talk? Write? Listen? Do you make other people feel good? If so, you've got what employers are looking for.

2. Intelligence

"Uh oh," you say. "Here comes my grade point average back to haunt me." There's little doubt that employers want intelligent people, but when we speak of intelligence, we don't necessarily mean the "brainy" type. (Colleagues of my generation will remember the guys in high school, pants hiked up to their armpits, slide rules firmly buckled to their belts. Naturally, they're the ones running Microsoft or basking in their jacuzzis out in the Silicon Valley these days.)

There are degrees and different types of intelligence. Many employers would love to hire intelligent high school graduates, intelligent secretaries who never went to college, and intelligent janitors who never went to high school. Employers are indeed aware of smarts, of street sense, of common sense.

Employers search for this kind of intelligence. Employers want someone who can understand an assignment, who can remember it, focus on it, and follow it through to completion. Employers want someone with ideas. Someone with originality. They want someone who can cut through the fog, see the gist of a problem, and set about solving it.

Employers are searching for these qualities, which they recognize as manifestations of intelligence. And they find what they want in plenty of people who cannot boast of a 3.0 grade point average (GPA).

Don't despair, all you Phi Beta Kappas and Ph.D.'s. Without a doubt, employers are looking for you, too. In the technical and scientific fields, superior academic credentials rank at the top of employers' lists of requirements. Indeed, employment managers dance with glee when they find the candidate with superior intelligence, as well as the other qualities they want.

Of course, employers will flock to those fortunate few ranked at the top of their classes. But let's face it. We can say with certainty that only 10 percent of the entire college population ranks in the top 10 percent of their classes. Ditto, high school. Ditto, law school. Ditto, graduate business school. Indeed, only one out of four students ranks in the top 25 percent of the class. The rest of us mortals can breathe a sigh of relief. There just aren't many people who rank at the top of the class. That leaves plenty of job opportunities for the rest of us.

So if your GPA didn't quite reach the magic 3.0, don't throw in the towel. Just remember, the numbers are on your side: 90 percent of the entire student population does not rank in the top 10 percent of the class. Employers want intelligent people working for their organizations. But given the choice between a candidate who has a 4.0 but shows few of the other fifteen attributes and a candidate who has a 2.5 but shows lots of pizzazz in the other qualities, many employers would opt for the second candidate.

3. Self-Confidence

Employers don't want wimps. They don't want somebody who shuffles through life, somebody who never looks you in the eye, or somebody who constantly apologizes. Neither do they want arrogant types whose views of themselves far exceed reality. Somewhere between arrogance and wimpishness lies the quality of self-confidence. Employers want people with backbone, people who are willing to take a stand and defend it. They want people who have ideas and are willing to convince others of their merit; people who recognize their own worth and want to contribute it to the organization in exchange for a financial or professional reward.

You might legitimately ask, "How can I show my self-confidence to a prospective employer?" Well, as you continue to read this book, you're going to find out that putting your job search together is itself an exercise in self-confidence. You'll learn that effective self-marketing shows not only what you've done with your life but also what you have accomplished. The mere act of showing your accomplishments in your job search demonstrates self-confidence. The way you go about your search shows your self-confidence, as does your choice of the best paper for your resumes and cover letters. Even signing your name the right way with the right pen shows your self-confidence. Indeed, the entire successful job search shows your self-confidence. Thus, when you follow the guidelines in this book, the style and tone of your job-search campaign will project self-confidence.

Yet style and tone don't do the final job of conveying your self-confidence—they lead the way for you to communicate the nature of your experiences, abilities, and accomplishments. Employers see self-confidence in professionals and managers who have made a difference in their organizations by leading their peers, changing a system, or reaching important goals. They also see it in college or high school students who work one or more summers away from home, who independently earn money to travel extensively in the U.S. or abroad, who develop a new way of taking inventory in a shoe store, or who hold a job for the same company for more than one summer. In short, you don't say in your resume, "I'm self-confident." Your experience and your approach show it.

4. Willingness to Accept Responsibility

Employers want people who recognize that a task needs to be done and then go about getting it done. Employers are looking for people who will volunteer to tackle the difficult job, indeed, people who love the challenge of the hard job. Employers also want people who are willing to take on the thankless tasks, who are willing to pay their dues, who know that successfully tending to boring chores often leads to more thrilling responsibilities. This idea, of course, applies not only to the trainee or junior employee, but also to middle- and upper-level managers and professionals who find themselves temporarily in less than ideal situations.

Employers don't want buck passers. Employers seek people who will admit their mistakes and repair any damage they cause. Employers want people who respond positively and maturely to criticism. They are looking for those who want their work evaluated and critiqued by others more in the know. They want people who desire to improve their performance and who know they can do it more quickly and effectively by paying attention to critical comment.

5. Initiative

As employers ourselves, we rank this quality near the top of our list. Employers want self-starters—people who can learn an overall operation and then work within it with little or no supervision; people who not only self-start, but who keep going from beginning to end.

6. Leadership

Just as your GPA represents an assessment of your intelligence by the combined opinion of your professors, your leadership experience represents an assessment of your character by the combined opinion of your peers. And, just as only 10 percent of the entire student population can rank in the top 10 percent of the class, the number of presidents is limited by the total number of groups that elect them. The total number of committee chairs is limited by the total number of committees. The number of editors-in-chief is limited by the number of student newspapers and yearbooks.

There are only so many chiefs out there. But keep in mind that recruiters for big corporations, government agencies, or public-service groups are not necessarily out to recruit the next Big Cheeses of their organizations. Sure, they are looking for people who one day might be the big honcho. They are looking for people who display leadership qualities. But they know only too well that not everyone can be the top person.

If you have never been elected president or vice president or secretary or treasurer, named foreman, or appointed chairperson, do not despair. Recruiters know that leadership qualities often bloom later in life, in the twenties, thirties, forties, fifties, and beyond. They also know of many Big People On Campus who have gone bust.

Undoubtedly, however, employers are also looking for evidence of leadership. When they recruit for their management training programs, they are trying to find the future leaders of their companies. So if you've already made your mark as a leader and shown strength in other attributes as well, you can rest assured your efforts will be rewarded. If, on the other hand, you're letting life slip by, perhaps it's time to get involved in some activities and try your hand at motivating and guiding your peers.

7. Energy Level

Employers are looking for people who know what hard work is all about. They seek people who don't poop out, people who are accustomed to work, who relish it, and who don't complain about how hard their jobs are. This attribute can be an advantage of the less verbal, less showy middle manager, salesperson, or professional. It can give the low-GPA graduating student or the person who hasn't been involved in many activities the chance to shine. Perhaps the low GPA is due to working twenty hours per week during school. Perhaps the tendency not to join a fraternity, sorority, or club is attributable to a lack of funds.

Believe us when we say recruiters will open their eyes wide when they see evidence of someone making money the old-fashioned way. They will welcome the thought of employing a graphic designer, for example, who produced quality work for several different clients over a short time, or a student who held several summer jobs simultaneously, someone who worked during school, someone who paid for a substantial part of his or her education costs.

If you're already a hard worker, you might indeed have a leg up on the preppie who spends summers checking his stocks on the Big Board as he leaps out of bed every day at the crack of noon. Yes, there still is room for the modern-day Horatio or Hortense Alger, and recruiters will know them when they see them.

8. Imagination

Although it's closely linked to intelligence, imagination denotes more than the common sense or street sense we spoke of above. Employers look for the people who can find solutions to problems, especially the problems that often have no common, textbook solutions.

Employers want innovators, creative people; they want what once was called the idea man—what we can call the idea person. Employers seek entrepreneurial talent, creative people whose minds naturally generate ideas, people who imagine solutions to problems—who can't imagine not finding a solution.

According to creativity guru Charles Chic Thompson in his book *What a Great Idea!* (New York, HarperCollins, 1992):

> Creativity is not a trait monopolized by a few fortunate souls. Every person is creative, because creativity is the trait that makes us human. Creativity is just another way to describe intelligence. To be creative is to have intelligence, to be able to gather information, and to make decisions based on that information. To be creative is to be able to perceive and recognize the world around us, to understand what we need or wish to do in response to it, and to set about changing it. To be creative is to find a way, a thought, an expression, a human manifestation no one else has found and to bring newly discovered possibilities into reality.

Everyone is creative, or at least has the innate potential to come up with great ideas. Look back in your experience and find those sparks of creativity employers seek.

9. Flexibility

Employers want people who can adapt to different situations. They do not want people limited by one way of thinking. They do not want people rigidly set in their ways. Instead, they look for people who are capable of changing, people who are receptive to new ideas and situations, people who can effectively evaluate a variety of opinions on how to perform a task.

They prefer the programmer, for example, who isn't reluctant to move out of a familiar niche to a new kind of software application; the executive who has shown the ability to alternate between different areas, such as sales and marketing and line management; the teacher who has also filled another related role, such as administrator, editor, or sales representative for educational products. Flexible combinations such as these, which straddle varied but related areas, often produce the most dynamic, fastest-advancing careers.

For graduating students, perhaps your having lived in various parts of the country shows your flexibility. Perhaps your travel abroad shows your adaptability. Perhaps your job one summer digging ditches and the next summer working as an aide in the state legislature shows how you can successfully function with a variety of people.

10. Interpersonal Skills

I hate this term *interpersonal skills*, I don't know why, I just do. I guess the term *skills* conjures up images of someone actually practicing how to get along with other people, perhaps even in front of a mirror. It's a term that seems to be accepted, by most everyone. It keeps cropping up. I guess I'll have to live with it.

What this term means is this: Someone who possesses these skills is capable of getting along with other people and making other people feel good about themselves. Someone blessed with these skills (or perhaps someone who has practiced them?) probably has a pleasant personality and a healthy self-image.

These are the basics. On a higher level, this trait translates to the ability to negotiate the many differences and frictions, stresses and strains, that always crop up between personalities, whether in conferences with customers and clients, brainstorming sessions with colleagues, board meetings, or project reviews. It means, for one thing, the ability to project one's own ideas without having to belittle or attack the views, or personalities, of others.

In this sense of the term, employers definitely want people who have interpersonal skills. Do you think employers want to hire someone with a rotten disposition? Do executives want to hire as colleagues someone they wouldn't really like to talk to? Does the office manager want someone who spends more time gossiping than getting the work done, someone who's a back-biter, or someone who never smiles? Do you think employers want to hire, whether on a junior, middle, or senior level, a boo-leader? Do you think they want an employee who constantly complains, who's out only for himself or herself, who worries incessantly about the other person's success and will go to almost any length to prevent it?

No, employers don't want those people. They want positive people who make other people feel good about themselves and about their company or organization. They're looking for employees who bring out the best in other people, who convey a positive and upbeat image of themselves and, consequently, the company.

Though we hate to use the term, we're convinced employers want people who have interpersonal skills.

11. Self-Knowledge

Employers watch out for those people who don't really know themselves. They are careful to avoid people with a lot of hang-ups, people whose self-images are far removed from reality. Employers are looking for people who can realistically assess their own capabilities, who can see themselves as others see them.

Employers want to find people who have correctly concluded that they are right for a particular position or project. They will avoid those who come on too strong seeking a situation for which they are ill equipped.

If you'd like to strengthen your grip on your knowledge of your own career goals, personal preferences, and job requirements, follow the procedures in the next chapter to get better acquainted with yourself. You may want to sharpen and expand your ideas concerning what you like to do, and define what you're good at doing. Explore the type of living conditions you want, and think about where you want to live. Determine the importance of making money (and how much money) in your scheme of things. Of course, many people in the executive and professional ranks, as well as many veterans of the blue-collar workforce, have come to the answers to these issues already, often the hard way. If you do know all these things about yourself, you'll pick the right job. And you'll have the self-knowledge employers are looking for in the first place.

12. Ability to Handle Conflict

The ability to handle conflict provides the chance to use another fancy term. Try this on for size: stress management. Now that's a good one. Of course, since I'm the one who introduced it into this discussion, I can't complain about it. But I think it may be even better than interpersonal skills.

People who can handle conflict are those with good skills in stress management. This means they can take it, they can function under pressure. It means they don't go screaming from the room when things get a bit tough.

We're not describing people loaded up with all sorts of stress vitamins—who break out in a cold sweat dreaming up new ways to be less stressed. We don't mean people who get all lathered up when they wake up to a rainy day that ruins their early-morning twenty-mile run, which they read somewhere would make them less stressed. While this portrait may simply betray my prejudice against megavitamins and arduous exercise, it helps illustrate the idea that the people who can handle the sorts of conflicts that crop up in the workplace are people who understand that some stress is inevitable, and who can tolerate that stress with patience, humor, and an eye toward learning from it.

Whatever stress management means, companies want it. They want people who don't panic, who remain calm under pressure, who aren't easily flustered. They want people who don't get all out-of-joint if things don't exactly go their way.

13. Goal Achievement

Employers are looking for people who can identify goals, work toward those goals, and reach them. In the private sector, if you're on the production end of things, your goal is to make more things better for less money. On the sales side, your goal is to sell more things to generate more income. In the public sector, measurements are constantly taken, goals quantified, and budgets followed. Public or private, goals are everywhere.

If you've been in the working world for some time, then you should survey your experience and collect concrete examples of goal setting and goal getting, regardless of whether they're measurable in dollars. Prominently display these achievements on your resume. Success will surely come.

If you're a student, you might not have measured your own goals in dollars. They might have been getting admitted to a particular college, attaining a certain grade in a certain course, getting a particular summer job, entering and finishing a particular race, or tackling a particular project. Even if you didn't know it, you probably have been operating under some set of goals.

If you've been out of the workforce for some time because of family responsibilities, you should look to your community or school volunteer work and determine whether you've been operating under some set of goals. Perhaps you spearheaded a membership drive that resulted in a 25 percent increase in the number of new members. Perhaps you took charge of the marching band concession stand at the football games and increased sales by 35 percent. Look around. You'll probably find goals set and goals attained.

Of course, many goals don't involve numbers of any kind; many don't have a finish line; some don't have an obvious payoff. It's up to you to look through your experience for any goals you accomplished that can demonstrate your ability to get things done.

14. Competitiveness

In the business world the name of the game is competition. In government, many agencies openly compete with one another.

In public-service organizations, successful fundraising requires all-out competition with other organizations seeking finite resources.

Now there's the healthful kind of competition ("I love to win") and the unhealthful kind ("I love to see the other guy lose!"). I'm fairly certain employers would quickly spot the latter type of competitor and conclude that he or she lacks the required interpersonal skills.

Competition is important, but I'm afraid many employers have decided there is only one kind of competition: athletic competition. Have you noticed how businesses climb all over themselves to get on the sports bandwagon? Have you noticed how McDonald's somehow equates the drive of Olympians with the drive to make a better Big Mac? And what on earth does 7-Eleven, a place where you can get a Twinkie at 3:00 in the morning, have to do with world-class cyclers? Surely anybody with a grain of sense knows competitive runners breaking the four-minute mile don't drink Lite-Beer-From-Miller-Everything-You-Always-Wanted-In-A-Beer-And-Less!

I remember well an interview with a law firm I had back in the 1970s. Here's the question I got from a senior partner of a respected firm: "Mr. Good, tell me, what has been your athletic background. We've found that those who succeed on the playing field undoubtedly will succeed in the courtroom." Well, in those days I didn't know the tricks I know now. I should have looked Mr. Jones squarely in the eye and said: "Mr. Jones, I'm not an athlete. I preferred to compete in the classroom instead."

You've probably gathered by now that I'm no jock. But knowing what I know about the apparent importance of sports, I'll tell you this: jocks, if you've got it, flaunt it. Right on your resume. If you lettered four years in varsity football, put it down on your resume. If you're an all-American basketball player, milk it for everything it's worth. If you captained the championship field hockey team, prominently display this fact on your resume. If you compete in marathons or triathlons, then make certain your future employer knows of your dedication, persistence, and prowess.

Now for the rest of us. If you're like us and your feet go one way when your brain commands them to go the other, that does not mean you lack competitive drive. And just because you'll never have the chance to sink a thirty-foot jumper with three seconds left on the clock doesn't mean you lack assertiveness. Indeed, some of the most competitive people we know literally have never reached first base. But metaphorically, they've hit home runs all their lives.

So nonjocks, show your competitive spirit as you've competed in the classroom. Show how you've competed politically. Show your zest for a good battle in the sales arena. There are plenty of places for all-out competition other than the playing field. Figure out those events in your life that show you like a good fight, you like to win, and you hate to lose.

15. Vocational Skills

If you're applying for a computer job, you'd better know computers. If you're applying for a position with a bank, you'd better like numbers. If you want to work for a newspaper, you'd better be able to write. Before you go out looking for a job, you've got to have the required skills. Employers don't want to spend a lot of money teaching you how to do what you should already know.

Let's take a moment to develop this point, for the benefit of readers who are just starting work, or who have children or nieces or nephews just starting out. We can already hear the recent graduate's lament. "I've only got a liberal arts degree," they cry. "I learned a lot in college and had a lot of fun. But jeez, they didn't teach me to *do* anything!"

Ah, but there you're wrong. Your experience as a student taught you to think. It taught you to solve problems, analytical problems and practical problems. Your experience in high school or college or graduate school taught you to communicate, to write, to speak, to stand on your feet. Life as a student taught you to be independent, to get along with other people, to resolve conflicts, to persuade others, to lead others, to accept or at least consider the views of others. If you went to college, then college life weaned you from Mom and Dad. During your college experience you arrived as a child and left, one hopes, as an adult.

Let's face it: you learned a great deal in college. And when you present yourself to employers, when you write your resume, you need to remember this and look for any tangible ways that this learning translates into achievements or skills. But there's no getting around it, today's world is highly technical. The business manager must be able to read and understand a financial statement, to know the difference between fixed and variable costs, to forecast sales, to project expenses, to hire the right people, to rent the right space at the right location, to bargain with the union, to order the right computer printout, and the list goes on and on.

So if you think your liberal arts degree left you lacking in specific skills, get going and sign up for some night courses or summer courses. Indeed, at many universities around the country business schools conduct summer institutes for unemployed Ph.D.'s. So for the person with a B.A. who feels a distinct lack of vocational skills, here are some words of wisdom from Longfellow: "It's time to be up and doing."

16. Direction

We reach the end of our list of attributes and find *direction*. This trait describes people who have defined their personal and professional needs. Employers want people who know what they want in life and why, for these are people who will work toward their goals, and find ways to harmonize their goals with the organization's. These people know what kind of employment position will mesh with their knowledge, skills, and personal desires.

By honestly assessing yourself, you should be able to define the work you want, the type of company or organization you want to work for, and where in the country you want to live. Those are all part of direction. And even though it's bound to change in the next five to ten years, it's important to have a direction now and follow it up by pursuing the right job with the right company, organization, or government agency in the right city.

These sixteen attributes were identified by a survey of the major corporate employers in the United States. Other evidence shows similar corporate desires. For example, a letter from a major recruiter to a college placement office outlines exactly what the company looks for in its new employees: Oral Communication, Job Motivation, Planning and Organizing, Attention to Detail, Leadership, Analysis, Stress Tolerance, Initiative, Practical Learning, Energy, Decision Making, Career Ambition, and Persuasiveness. As another example, a very large American corporation equips its interviewers with a rating sheet that lists these criteria to use in ranking the applicants: Adaptability, Career Preparation, Job-Related Knowledge and Skills, Communication Skills, Leadership, and Energy Level.

Honesty and Speed: Attributes for the 1990s

We should expand the above list with two more attributes that business and government must seek in the 1990s. One is honesty. Hardly a month goes by when the national news isn't announcing the latest scandal to rock Wall Street, Congress, Main Street, or the media itself. Brokers are convicted in insider-trading scandals. Senators are involved in the savings and loan scandal. Top banking officials rip off unsuspecting depositors. A journalist must return a Pulitzer Prize for having fabricated a story about drug addiction among children. A music group must return its Grammy Award for not having actually performed the material released under its name.

Companies are acutely aware of the problem of honesty. This means, for example, that they know all about the problem of resume fraud. They know that people tend to fudge on their resumes. Some people lie outright on their resumes. To counter the problem, many employers commission investigative services to verify the facts portrayed on applicants' resumes! Hence the two rules for resume writers:

1. Never fabricate information on a resume.
2. Try to show affirmatively your traits of honesty and integrity.

Each of these deserves separate comment. First, while you should never put false information on your resume, neither should you include damaging information. Thus, if you were fired from a job, don't say you "left to obtain a more challenging position," because it's a false statement. But also don't say you were fired. What do you say? You say nothing. You have no ethical obligation to reveal damaging information on your resume. However, if you are asked in an interview why you left that particular job, you must be forthright.

Second, if you've held positions of trust, make a point of showing your honesty and integrity. For example, if you handled money as a sales clerk or bank teller, make sure your resume says you "handled large sums of cash, accurately accounting for every penny."

Now, another attribute for the 1990s: speed. One sign of the times: Jack Welch, chief executive officer of General Electric, recently instituted WorkOut, a new mindset for all of GE's operations, which seeks to inject "speed, simplicity, and self-confidence" into the workplace. All GE employees—managers and factory workers alike—are attending special training programs to implement WorkOut companywide across the globe. As part of the same trend, John Young, chief executive officer of Hewlett-Packard, made it a corporate goal to cut in half the time between a product's conception and its profitability.

Both businesses and public-sector organizations must speed up their operations if they are to compete effectively in the coming decade. You should seriously evaluate your own speed and simplicity in getting things done.

To show you just how important the trait of speed is, I'll just ask you to think about the last time you were in a checkout line at a grocery store and the clerk was going oh . . . so . . . slowly, that it just about drove you bats. Will that clerk succeed? Will that store succeed with those kinds of clerks? No way.

Friendly, Courteous, Kind . . .

Take a careful look at your marketing survey. Do the traits sound familiar? Sure. They're all looking for the same thing: a Boy Scout or Girl Scout—someone who is trustworthy, loyal, helpful, friendly, courteous, kind, obedient, cheerful, brave, clean, and reverent. We're exaggerating, of course. But you should have no doubt that companies know what they want. Now you must show that you've got precisely that.

CHAPTER 2

Of Resumes That Wear Blue Jeans

Keys to Successful Self-Marketing

YOU KNOW WHAT EMPLOYERS want from you. Now you need to study your product and see how to package it to cater to the consumer's desires. In doing so, you'll avoid the chief mistake of most job seekers, which is to dress their qualifications and accomplishments in the plainest, poorest way possible—like showing up at a job interview dressed in dingy old blue jeans.

That's what I used to do, until one of my students set me straight one day. I remember it well, since it was not only the starting point for this book but a turning point in my legal career at the time. I was in my office at the University of Virginia School of Law reviewing my resume and essay, which I was about to submit to the Supreme Court of the United States to apply for a Judicial Fellowship. It was a Friday. The application was due Monday.

As I was about to seal the envelope and send it off to the Supreme Court, a law student poked his head in my office and asked, "What're ya doing, Mr. Good?" I told him and invited him in. We discussed the fellowship I was itching to get, and I described how meticulous I had been with my resume, essay, and all the other stuff.

"Mind if I take a look?" he asked.

"Of course not," I said and handed it over.

After taking one look at my resume, the color drained from his face. Mustering every ounce of tact a law student can muster (which isn't a whole helluva lot), he said, "Ed, this is awful!"

"Whaddya mean 'awful'?"

"Wait here," he said, as if I had something more important to do than find out why my resume was awful.

"Take a look at this," he said, pulling out his resume, a note of triumph in his voice. I took a look. Now the color drained from my face, replaced immediately by the green of envy. His resume was beautiful. Mine, without doubt, was awful. My resume wore blue jeans. His didn't; it was properly dressed. His caught the reader's eye and forced him to see the credentials he wanted to emphasize. It was graphically designed, whereas mine was thrown together.

"Most people create a mess when they put their resumes together," he said. "If I were you, I'd change yours like this." And he showed me how to create a work of art.

Fortunately, my resume was stored on an IBM mag card typewriter in the typing pool of the law school. I gave my student's revisions to the mag card operator and, within minutes, had a terrific resume neatly attached to my application materials. Off they went to the Supreme Court.

The fellowship? I won. After a year in Washington I returned to Virginia Law School to teach legal writing for two more years. Then I resigned to start my own business, which specialized in resume and direct mail services for job seekers all over the United States. Since we began in 1980, we've prepared thousands of resumes for college students, business students, medical, law, and other graduate students, and professionals from all parts of the country.

That experience led to publication of the earlier incarnation of this book. While running that business, which I have since sold, I saw everything there is to see in resumes and job-search strategies from just about every type of person. I saw an architect's resume designed like a blueprint. I saw another typeset in sixteen different typefaces. I met the student who wanted to print his resume on special paper bearing the picture of a shade tree.

As my firm gained substantial experience in the field, and as our resumes began to be noticed by employers and college placement directors, I was asked to conduct workshops in resume preparation as my colleague, Bill Fitzpatrick, does on military bases throughout the world. In those workshops we've responded to just about every conceivable question people can have about producing their resumes. We've accumulated a wealth of experience and seen many examples of the pitfalls people encounter when they prepare their resumes and launch their job searches.

We constantly face the tendency people have to sell themselves short. We've coached the young man who wondered whether he should include on his resume his brief experience as a player with the National Football League. We've counseled the young woman who was tempted to leave out her numerous awards showing horses at Madison Square Garden. We've encouraged and then applauded the professional woman who took the first, uncertain steps toward a major job change and then plowed straight ahead toward the success she deserves. We've guided innumerable job and career searches that had been stuck in blue jeans when they needed and deserved to be in much bolder, more self-assertive attire.

Restyling Your Self-Presentation

As you take a look at yourself, at your life, you must change out of your mental blue jeans: you absolutely must keep at the forefront of your thinking those attributes the employers are seeking. You must conclude that yes, indeed, your experiences demonstrate those attributes the employers want. Thus, you've got to look not only at what you've done but also at what you've accomplished.

We're going to demonstrate the process by example, using sample resume entries for illustration, but the principle I applied here also applies to every other aspect of your self-presentation in the job search. We'll follow the same process for graduating students, professionals, others already in the workforce, and homemakers reentering the workforce.

Graduating Students

During your assessment of yourself, which we've outlined below, you might be thinking back to one of your summer jobs. You remember. The summer when you waited tables at Bill's Bar and Grill during the day and did volunteer work for the rescue squad at night. The typical resume attired in blue jeans would describe this job as follows:

> Waiter, Bill's Bar and Grill, Inc., Chattanooga, TN, Summer 1989. Waited tables and helped in the kitchen.

That resume flunks! Keep in mind what the employer wants. A waiter? A kitchen helper? No, the employer wants people with interpersonal skills, stress management skills, energy level, and adaptability. So you think back about that job and realize that you served truckers at Bill's Bar and Grill, a truck stop on a busy interstate highway. And as you think back, you realize that you handled those ornery truckers pretty well, that you often had to remember many orders simultaneously, that you handled their complaints positively and calmly. Then you realize that you worked fifty hours a week at Bill's and twenty more hours a week at the rescue squad at night. It then begins to dawn on you that you exhibited stress management, interpersonal skills, adaptability, and a high energy level—you worked your tail off that summer.

Keeping those attributes in mind you write a winning resume entry like this:

> Employment: Bill's Bar and Grill, Chattanooga, Tennessee.
> Waited tables serving interstate truckers in a fast-paced truck stop. Responded positively and calmly to any customer complaints. Worked 50 hours per week while simultaneously volunteering 20 hours per week to the local rescue squad. Summer 1989.

Note that, while you didn't use the terms stress management, interpersonal skills, adaptability, or energy level, those are the precise messages you conveyed on your resume. Remember, the employer is no dummy. She knows what she wants, and she will get the message. You showed the employer you're adaptable (you're seeking a white-collar job but worked well in a blue-collar environment), you managed stress and got along extremely well with people (fast-paced restaurant, calmly responding to complaints), and you worked hard (seventy hours a week).

Homemakers Reentering the Workforce

During your assessment of yourself, which we have outlined on page 31, you might be thinking about the extensive volunteer work you used to do before you had children. You remember. You cranked up a used clothing consignment store to raise money for the local rescue squad. The resume that wears blue jeans would describe the experience as follows:

> Centerville Rescue Squad, Centerville, NC.
> Volunteered to raise funds by selling used clothes on consignment. 1981–84.

Does the employer want a used clothes salesperson? No, the employer wants people with interpersonal skills, stress management skills, energy level, initiative, and leadership ability. So you think about that four-year project and realize that you started an enterprise from scratch, handled all the publicity, developed an inventory control system to keep track of consignors and the amounts of money due, and recruited and led other volunteer workers. As you think back, you realize that the project earned nearly $25,000 per year for the local rescue squad. It then begins to dawn on you that you exhibited interpersonal skills, stress management skills, energy level, initiative, and leadership ability. Keeping those attributes in mind, you write an excellent resume entry as follows:

Managerial   Centerville Rescue Squad, Centerville, NC
Experience: Single-handedly started a clothing consign-
                ment store to raise funds for the county rescue
                squad. Procured donated space from a local mer-
                chant, recruited and supervised 12 volunteers,
                and obtained free publicity on television and
                radio. Operated the store for four straight years,
                earning nearly $100,000 for the rescue squad.
                Devised a unique record-keeping system to track
                items by consignors and to pay them their share of
                the proceeds of sale. Dealt directly and effectively
                with members of the public. 1981–84.

Here again you didn't use the terms interpersonal skills, stress management skills, energy level, initiative, or leadership ability, but those are the attributes this resume conveys. By writing for your future employer, you showed you can manage stress (no one starts a business without confronting and handling stress), lead others (training twelve volunteers), develop new systems (creating the consignor control system), and get along with people (dealing directly with the public).

Professionals and Managers

Here's how the process might apply to people already in mid-career. During your self-assessment, which we've outlined next, you might be thinking about your experience as sales manager when you took over a territory after performing extremely well as an up-and-coming salesman. The typical, blue-jeans-clad resume would describe the experience as follows:

Employment: ACME Widgets, Midtown, Oklahoma
                Sales Manager. Responsible for other sales
                representatives.

Now that's awful. Does the employer want someone who is "responsible for other sales representatives," or someone who gets results? The employer wants people with interpersonal skills, stress management skills, energy level, initiative, and leadership ability. So you think back about that sales manager's job and remember that you were elevated rather rapidly from salesperson to assistant sales manager to sales manager. You remember that as a sales representative you increased your sales by 150 percent after one year, that you advanced rapidly, that the sales force you led typically outperformed other sales groups in other parts of the country. It then begins to dawn on you that you exhibited all the skills the employer seeks. Next is the more impressive resume entry:

Sales Experience: **ACME Widgets,** Midtown, Oklahoma, 1984–1989
Served as a Manufacturer's Representative for two years serving widget accounts throughout the Southeast. During the second year, increased total sales by 150%. Because of success, advanced to Assistant Sales Manager and then quickly to Sales Manager.

- *Sales Management.* Directed and supervised a team of eight Sales Representatives serving the southeast territory. Motivated and trained each team member.
- *Sales Quotas.* Consistently ranked as the Number One sales team for the entire country. Increased territory sales by 25% each year for three consecutive years.
- *Sales Meetings.* Designed a new Sales Meeting Agenda, complete with visual aids, that was adopted for use by all other sales territories.

Here, you've conveyed to your future employer that you can manage stress (no one succeeds in sales without confronting and handling stress), lead others (you trained eight sales reps), develop new systems (you created the new sales meeting agenda), and get along with people (you dealt directly with clients).

If you've forgotten the attributes, go back right now to Chapter 1 and write down the sixteen qualities employers want in their employees. Keep the list handy, because you're about to create some lists about yourself as you take a trip down nostalgia lane.

Take a Deep Breath . . .

Are you ready? Probably not; you likely have some doubts about this. You're probably saying, "Jeez, these guys are trying to teach me to be an arrogant so-and-so. I can't write a resume and brag about myself. Don't they know humility is a virtue? How can I possibly make that job slinging hash sound like a study in customer relations at the Harvard Business School?"

Let us quell your doubts. For simplicity, let's use the Bill's Bar and Grill example above. You should not be arrogant, but neither should you be a shrinking violet. (Employers want someone who is self-confident, right?) Certainly you've accomplished something in your life. Did you or did you not deal effectively with customers when you were slinging hash at Bill's? If you did, you should say so. If you didn't, if you constantly haggled with the customers, and even came to blows with those burly truckers, then maybe we can rephrase it to show you were "assertive with unruly clientele." Or maybe you should leave out your customer relations skills altogether and focus on your "successful operation of the cash register" and your "responsibility to make night deposits exceeding $2,000."

The point is that in almost every job, activity, sport, and course you've taken, in fact, in almost everything you've done, you've accomplished something worthwhile. You've done something that shows you have the traits employers want. As we'll discuss in Chapter 3, you've got perhaps thirty seconds of the employer's time when she reviews your resume. Your task is to show what you have accomplished in your life, and these accomplishments must prove you've got the right stuff.

You won't find an ad saying, "We think we've got a pretty good toothpaste. Give it a try. Maybe you'll like it." But that's the same message as, "Waited tables and helped in the kitchen." What employer in her right mind wants to hire a waiter and a kitchen helper to participate in a highly expensive management training program? Not any employers we know, except maybe the one in Chattanooga at a place called Bill's Bar and Grill. If that's the job you want, go for it.

But consider this as well. Remember attribute Number 11, self-knowledge. If you overpuff in your resume, if you put a fifty dollar saddle on a mule and try to call it a show horse, then the employer can rightly conclude that you lack self-knowledge. Let's face it, you want a tasteful resume, not an ad for Fast Eddie's Used Cars or even a toothpaste commercial. You have to find the happy medium between arrogance and wimpishness. Thus, the next task before writing your ad is to analyze your product. Get ready. Toss your humility out the window and take the following trip of self-assessment.

Go Blow Your Horn

1. Find a quiet place where you can be alone. Be sure to take along a legal pad. And don't forget, leave your humility behind.

2. Tear off four sheets of paper from the legal pad. At the top of the first, write, "Education." At the top of the second, write, "Things I've Done for Pay." At the top of the third, write, "Things I've Done for Free." At the top of the fourth, write, "Things I Like to Do and Have Done Well."

3. Education Page.
   a. College and graduate students. On the Education page, write down the names of the colleges and graduate schools you've attended, their cities and states or countries, and the dates you attended. Write down the degrees you received or expect to receive. Write down the dates of your degrees or anticipated degree. Now here's a real mental exercise for you: write down all courses you've taken. Write down the subjects or titles of any papers you've written. Write

down your cumulative GPA, your GPA in your major, your GPA in the last two years, your GPA in the last year. Write down your SAT scores, GRE scores, LSAT scores, or any other relevant scores on academic ability tests.

b. High school students. Follow the same procedure. Write down the name and city of your high school, the courses you took, the grades you made, the papers you wrote, the standardized tests you took, and the scores you made.

c. Professionals, managers, and homemakers reentering the workforce. You might have attended college centuries ago. Don't worry about remembering your courses or term papers or grades. For many adults at this stage of life, educational information is almost irrelevant for resume purposes. Just cover the basics, adding anything that might be unusually interesting (for example, if you're an editor and you founded a magazine during school, or you're a manager and you launched a successful legitimate business while attending college).

4. On the Things-I've-Done-for-Pay page, write down the names of every employer you've had and the positions you've held. If your job really didn't have an official position name, then make one up that accurately and honestly describes the type of work you did. For each job, write down everything you did, your actual tasks. Also write down the beginning and ending dates for each job you held. Now, and most important, write down what you achieved at each job. (Review Chapter 1 and the list of sixteen attributes.) What did you do that shows you have what the employers are looking for? Did you work hard? If so, how many tasks did you handle or how many hours did you work per week? Did you come up with new ways of doing things? Did you handle money? If so, how much each day, how much each week, how much over the entire course of your job? Did you do any writing? Did you help train anybody else?

If so, how many people? Did you supervise any other people? If so, how many? Did you work effectively as a member of a team? Did you reach any goals or objectives? Did you set any records? Think now. What did you achieve? How did you make a difference?

Professionals, managers, and homemakers reentering the workforce need to account for employment experience only back to the time you were graduated from college. If some of your early positions are not career related, they will simply be listed on your resume to account for that time period. For your career-related work, you want to follow the procedure I just described to get a handle on your marketable achievements.

5. On the Things-I've-Done-for-Free page, write down every group or organization you've been affiliated with since the tenth grade in school. Jot down any offices you held. Were you elected? Selected? If so, out of how many applicants? Include a brief description of what you did with these groups. What were your accomplishments? Again, keep the sixteen attributes in mind. Also on this page, write down any honors or awards you've received. Be sure you include parenthetically next to each honor or award a brief description of what the honor or award represented. What quality did the honor or award recognize? How many others received the award? What was the size of the population from which the winners of the honor or award were chosen? Again, take a hard look at this page. Look at your activities, your honors, your awards, and your community service. What attribute in you was recognized by these awards or honors? What quality did you display by participating in these activities? We cannot stress enough how important it is that your resume not only summarize what you did but also what you accomplished and what qualities you demonstrated.

6. Take out the page entitled "Things I Like to Do and Have Done Well." Think back to high school and remember what you did. Do the same for college. Focus on any

aspects of your life. Just list what you like to do. Describe your major conquests, the things you've done the best.

Now comes the hard part. Compare the Pay page, the Free page, and the Like-to-Do page. Is the information on all three pages similar? If so, you can conclude that you are a well-directed person, doing what you like to do. You like your work. You like your activities. You like your rewards for your accomplishments. Good for you. You have "direction."

But if the information on the three pages differs, don't despair. Perhaps this means you've had to take jobs you didn't particularly like for financial reasons. That could mean you're adaptable and hard-working. If your Like-to-Do page totally differs from your Pay and Free pages, perhaps that means you have well-rounded, uniquely appealing interests that should appear on your resume.

7. Look over the Pay, Free, and Like-to-Do pages. Do you see any patterns? Are there any attributes that appear on all three pages? For example, if you wrote on the Like-to-Do page that you enjoy writing, on the Pay page that you held a job as a copy editor on a newspaper, and on the Free page that you served as a reporter on your college newspaper, then you're well on your way to deciding what kind of resume you should have. If you don't see much overlap, then you too are well on your way to deciding what kind of resume you should have (as shown in the next chapter).

8. Take out another sheet of paper and write, "References," at the top. List any people in your entire life (no relatives!) who would blow their horns for you. List their titles, such as president, manager, or professor. Look over the list of names. If any of these people is recognizable by name, for example, a well-known national or local leader, then you might decide to use him or her as a reference on your resume. Look over the list of titles. If the titles are impressive, you might decide

to use these people as references, too. Begin to locate current addresses and telephone numbers. In a later chapter we'll discuss ways to deal with references on your resume.

9. Take out your Pay page and look over your positions. List them chronologically, the most recent listed first. When you've completed the list, look down it and see if you find any position that is more impressive than the first-listed. Put a big red circle around the more impressive positions. Can you identify these more impressive positions as being in a particular subcategory of employment? For example, can you portray these more impressive positions as writing experience, sales experience, computer experience, or any other category you can dream up? If so, write this subcategory in large letters next to these more impressive positions.

Money, Location, Job

One other form of self-quiz is essential to your job search at this stage, especially if you're a professional or manager. You need to develop a plan for what you hope to achieve in your job search. Without it, you may be severely lacking in the critical area of self-knowledge.

Before you even start to plan a program to find that meaningful position, it's a good idea to review what's important to you in your life. If you know your goals, you can conceive a plan that will help you realize those goals. There really are only three major goals to consider in your professional life: money, location, and job (or position). There probably are many more subgoals, but they generally fit into one of these three. Most people are not able to realize all three goals simultaneously; one or two of the goals have to be sacrificed, and some priorities have to be set.

An excellent example of money-location-job choices that could apply in many different kinds of situations is the story of a lieutenant colonel friend who was leaving the service after twenty-three years. He had been smart with his investments and was going to be able to count on some regular income after retirement. He also owned his home, which had been purchased during an early assignment, and he planned on moving there immediately after leaving the service. He had two children in high school, and he felt that if he could find a job paying $35,000 per year, he would only have to work ten more years. That would allow his children time to finish school. Then he would be situated well enough financially that he could retire.

This fellow seemed to have some real goals established (money), and he knew what he wanted to do. But the house he was planning to move into was in Lawton, Oklahoma, just outside of Fort Sill. We had to wonder how many salaried positions in Lawton, Oklahoma, pay $35,000 per year. Not many, we guessed, unless the colonel could find a position in commissioned sales. Then he could control his own income. Otherwise, he had set himself up for some real frustration.

His real goal was location, not money. The house, and not his need to retire early, was driving his decision. He didn't realize most jobs that pay the kind of money he needed were not to be found in small communities, but in major metropolitan areas.

In another example, an army sergeant major living in the midwest also thought he had it all figured out. He had spent many years in the recruiting field and had also obtained a degree in Marketing, through off-duty college courses. His only goal was to get into the marketing business. He truly enjoyed the pace, the creativity, and the fulfillment he believed he'd receive from a successful marketing campaign. He began to float his resume around the country, and after several inquiries received a call from a company in the San Francisco Bay Area. The vice president was quite impressed with the sergeant major and, after a long telephone interview, invited him to the home office for a final meeting. If all went well, he had the job.

Upon arriving home that evening the sergeant major told his wife about the phone call and asked her help in getting ready to travel to the Bay Area the following week. He needed a suit and a new briefcase, and had to do some research on the company.

His, wife, however, objected. "Look," she said, "I've been following you around for over twenty years. Every time I got a decent job with some hope for advancement, you got transferred and I had to quit. Our children have been in five different schools and are still in high school. I have a pretty good job here, and I have a chance of getting promoted into management. We're living in the first house we have ever owned, and I like it. If you think I'm packing up and moving to San Francisco or some other place, you're crazy." The sergeant major soon found that it wasn't position that was going to direct his job-search efforts, but location.

Ask Yourself Some Questions

The real question you have to ask yourself is what you are willing to give up. Will you sacrifice that perfect job in order to live in a hospitable climate? Will you accept a little less money for just the right job? Only you, aided by discussion with family, can make a final decision. Here are some questions that should help you reach that decision.

Do you want to work in your current specialty? _____

Do you own a home that you will remain in? _____

Are your children still living at home and still in school? _____

How much money do you need? _____

How much money would you like to make? _____

Do you have the qualifications to make that much money? _____

Do you want to supervise people? _____

Would you move to another part of the country for the right offer? _____

Could you live in a small town? _____

Could you live in a big city? _____

Do you plan on continuing your education? _____

Does your spouse have a good job? _____

Would your spouse quit and move? _____

Can you stand a high-stress job? _____

Do you know where you want to be professionally
in five years? _____

As you begin to work your way through these questions,
you will soon discover that in some cases you will wind up with
more than a *yes* or *no* answer, or perhaps no answer at all. That
should tell you something, too. In many cases you may wind
up with a *maybe* or a *possibly,* but don't let that stop you from
considering all of the possibilities. The purpose of the exercise
is to get you thinking and talking. Sound decisions will come
when you and your family have considered all of the possibilities. Remember, no one else can answer these questions for you;
even if you seek advice from other people, you have to face each
of them yourself. Before you can begin the job search, you must
know what is really important to you.

You've Only Just Begun

Don't for a minute think you've planned your job search or written your resume. You haven't. You've only taken some notes on
yourself. As the job-search procedure unfolds in later chapters,
you'll begin to see more clearly the form, content, and style your
ultimate job-search campaign will take. All you've done so far
is to research your consumer and your product. Now let's study
the three kinds of resumes. Then you can pick the most effective way to write your message to your future employer.

CHAPTER 3

Thirty Seconds of Air Time

The Importance of Your Resume

THE PROCESS OF FINDING the right job—of successfully selling your product—is basically no different from that of selling your car, your house, or anything else. It requires you to develop a marketing plan, create an advertisement, and use that ad to set the plan in motion, to let as many people as possible know you are available for work.

The advertisement, in this case, comes first, because it will be the centerpiece of your campaign. Writing your ad will be your means of defining, first for yourself and then for others, what you have to offer. Before you conduct your job search, you need a document that distills your qualifications and experience; this document not only becomes your advertising piece, it's your touchstone, a point of reference any time you have the opportunity to present yourself to a potential employer. It's the most important practical homework you'll do in preparation for your quest. It's a reminder, for you, of all the things you want to stress to your audience. It's the short, sweet version of all the self-presentations you'll make in your search. That document, that ad, of course, is your resume.

Why Do I Need a Resume?

Some people don't think they need one. Indeed, some experts counsel job seekers not to have resumes or to write something different from a resume. Such advice, we believe, is misguided, for the resume is traditionally the keystone of the American job search. Almost all classified ads say, "Send resume." All headhunters want a copy of your resume. All leads you uncover in your networking will say, "Send me a copy of your resume." Are you going to say you read a job-search book that's down on resumes and that, therefore, you don't have one? Good luck. If you're going after a significant position, you want to reach as many people as possible. The resume helps you do that effectively.

Your resume can serve as your calling card. It can function as a sales piece in a mass mailing campaign. It will accompany every letter you send out inquiring about employment possibilities or responding to an advertised position. Your resume will get the ball rolling.

The Definition of a Resume

We can best tell you what a resume is by telling you what it isn't. Your resume does not document your life. It doesn't drone on, in painful detail, boring the reader with your achievements such as "Chairperson of the High School Civitan Club's Car Wash Fundraising Committee, 4/79–5/79." It need not account for every job you've ever held. It certainly does not record your failures. Assuredly it omits those ho-hum interests you have in "Jogging, Reading, and Music." Likewise, your resume is not your birth certificate, so it'll probably omit your birthdate as well. Your resume is not your Social Security card. It doesn't proudly shout to the world, "I'm 123-45-6789!" And, unless you're Tom Cruise or Kim Basinger, your resume is not the cover of *Vanity Fair*. As a rule, no pictures.

The no-picture rule is subject to some debate. Some colleges or graduate schools have prescribed resume formats that require a picture. If you feel a picture will help your message, or if you must provide a picture to comply with a prescribed format, then get the best picture possible. Be prepared to spend some money with a professional photographer. Do not get a cheap passport photo! If you plan to have your photo printed on the resume (rather than attached), then get a black and white photo (not color), for it will produce a sharper image when printed. If you plan to attach a photo, then definitely get color pictures professionally done.

Your resume is not one of the Dead Sea scrolls. It should not be prepared on ancient, disintegrating paper. Neither should it appear on cheap onionskin complete with erasures. Your resume is not an eyesore. It is not full of visual distortions giving the employer a blinding headache as he searches through your tortured format for the essence of you.

A Thirty-Second
Toothpaste Commercial

Those are some of the things a resume is not. Therefore, it should be perfectly clear to you by now that a resume is a toothpaste commercial. That's right. A toothpaste commercial. Or at least it functions just like one.

Let us prove our point. Take out your watch, preferably your jogger's watch. The one that calculates time in thousandths of a second along with heartbeat, humidity, and altitude. That's the one. Have you got it? Okay. Let's do a test.

On the next page you'll find a resume, a typical one that wears blue jeans. Now, when we say "Go," begin reading this typical resume. Are you ready? Okay. "Go!"

1 . . . 2 . . . 3 . . . 4 . . . 5 . . . 6 . . . 7 . . . 8 . . . 9 . . . 10 . . . 11 . . . 12 . . . 13 . . . 14 . . . 15 . . . 16 . . . 17 . . . 18 . . . 19 . . . 20 . . . 21 . . . 22 . . . 23 . . . 24 . . . 25 . . . 26 . . . 27 . . . 28 . . . 29 . . . 30 . . . STOP!

The typical "Blue Jeans" resume.

R E S U M E

Hubert I. "Hubie" Jackson
Home address - 401 Main Street
     Apt.# 345-2A
     Springfield, Massachusetts 02139
Telephone: 617-234-4321

Date of Birth: 1/17/65
Health: Excellent
Availability: Immediate
Marital Status: Single

CAREER OBJECTIVE: A challenging and rewarding position in a company's Management TRaining Program.

EDUCATION: 9/1/83–6/6/87 BA History, St. Charles College
             4657 River Pike
             Springfield, Ma. 02345
    Courses: History 101, HIstory 102, History 103, History 104
            Economics 202
            Computers (Basic, Cobol, Pascal)

HONORS & AWARDS: Dean's List (1 semester)
                Alpha Alpha Chi History honorary fraternity
                --chairman, fundraising committee, 9/84-2/85
                --vice-chairman, fundraising committee, 9/83-3/84
                --also worked on the newsletter committee, 3/84-5/84
                The Tattler (school newspaper) -- sports page layout dept.
                --assisted editor and responsible for layout supervision

EMPLOYMENT: 6/1/83-8/30/83: Clerk Typist, AG Office, Commonwealth of
Massachusetts
            --general office duties in attorney general's office
            --responsible for some research and running errands
              (including filing papers in court)

            6/2/82-8/25/82: Clerk Typist, AG Office, Commonwealth of
Massachusetts
            --responsible for: typing court documents; helping in discovery pro-
ceedings; prepared reports; office management.

INTERESTS: Reading, Music, Jogging, All Sports.

EARLY BACKGROUND: Born and raised in Springfield, Massachusetts. Attended
                Springfield High School (valedictorian of senior class),
                Lettered 4 years on high school track team, winning state track
                meet in high hurdles. Elected president of student body.

REFERENCES: Available On Request.

Thirty-Second Scan Rule

You've finished.

"But," you say, "I haven't finished."

We know you haven't finished. But we can tell you this: *The prospective employer reviewing your resume has finished!* That's right. Prospective employers spend about thirty seconds reviewing your resume. Just thirty seconds. And if your resume wears blue jeans like the one you just didn't finish reading, there go your chances out the window. In thirty seconds your career hopes are dashed, your life crushed.

We didn't say it's fair. We're just telling you what actually happens when employers review resumes. So now you know your chances for that "stimulating position offering the chance to use my organizational and communication skills" are down the drain in thirty seconds flat. After you calm down from this devastating bit of news, you might more soberly ask, "But how can any sensible employer make important employment decisions in just thirty seconds? If that company makes decisions like that, I don't want to work there anyway." As you continue to think about it, you might even conclude that this guy who writes books about resumes wearing blue jeans has got to have a seam loose somewhere, too.

Let me defend my point and myself from your relentless attacks. Employers do not use resumes to make hiring decisions. They use resumes to make interviewing decisions. So add this important item to the list of what a resume isn't: *A resume does not get a job. A resume does get an interview!* Put yourself in the employer's position. How many resumes do you think a large company receives? For that matter, how extensively can the owner or president of a small company review the many resumes received each week? What do you think a personnel officer is going to do with several hundred resumes pouring in, in response to a classified ad? Are the personnel officer and the personnel staff going to study every resume? Furthermore, are they going to extend offers on the basis of a resume? Without talking to the person? Without checking references? No, they're not.

Your resume begins the process of showing how your features, as we discussed earlier, translate into benefits for an employer. Your resume, your ad, will not, however, get you a job. For example, if someone sees the ad for a car you're selling, we doubt he'll call you up and say, "Hey, this is exactly the car I'm looking for. Send it over and I'll have a check for you." More likely, the potential buyer will come over to look at the car first. He'll sit in the driver's seat, kick the tires, and then look under the hood and pretend he knows what's going on under there.

Meet the Employment Manager

The purpose of an advertisement is to create interest, to get someone to try the toothpaste or to come over and kick the tires. It should make someone want to see the product and then allow you the opportunity to sell it to them. The same principle applies to your job search. Your resume will spark some interest in prospective employers to call you for an interview, so that you can come in, all dressed up, and get *your* tires kicked. Sparking that interest isn't as easy as you might think. Let's look at the facts.

Your market is the human resources or employment manager, who doesn't have a lot of time to spend on your resume and is only interested in your qualifications and your ability to do the job. Although statistics vary, most personnel experts in large organizations would agree that the average employment manager reviews 20,000 resumes each year. Let's assume this overworked employment manager takes a two-week vacation each year. She thus has 400 resumes to review each week, or 80 each working day. During the working day this employment manager is traveling and conducting interviews. She's going to have to do her resume reading at night. Let's say she begins at 9:00 P.M.

There she is, facing a stack of eighty resumes. She picks up the first and sees it's a mess. The format makes her squint. The typing looks like it came from an antique Underwood typewriter, the kind with black and red cloth ribbons. "Hmmm," she muses, "sloppy guy." Ten seconds have elapsed. She hastily puts the first in the reject pile, even though buried in the resume was the interesting bit of news that the applicant had a 3.4 GPA at a respected university.

She moves quickly to the next resume. She knows what she's looking for. She begins each resume with a scan, looking for the attributes valued by her company. When she spots those attributes, her scan becomes a read. That resume caught her eye and forced her attention to the attributes she was looking for in the first place. That resume she puts in the let's-take-a-look pile.

Most of the resumes from her stack will end up in the reject pile, and some in that pile are undoubtedly the resumes of qualified candidates. But these candidates failed to understand what the employer was looking for and how to display their credentials to show they had exactly that.

In that first thirty-second screening you must wind up in the let's-take-a-look pile in order to have any chance of getting that important interview. Almost 75 percent of the resumes received in response to advertising are discarded. These people never receive an invitation for an interview. After the in-depth review, a much smaller number of candidates get invited for an interview, maybe as many as 10 percent, but more likely, as few as 1 percent.

A company that runs an advertisement for a significant position in a major metropolitan Sunday newspaper can generally expect to receive up to one hundred replies. They sometimes receive as many as one thousand. They can really only interview somewhere in the neighborhood of ten people for the position. That means that between 90 percent and 99 percent of the respondents will never be called. Your job is to figure out how to be one of those 1 percent to 10 percent who get the call.

Our average employment manager might be responsible for hiring about 200 people per year. If she receives 20,000 resumes per year, then only one out of one hundred is going to be hired. Also, in this typical organization she might interview three to five candidates for each position. This means only three to five resumes out of one hundred are going to result in an interview. As our employment manager goes about tackling her rather large pile of resumes, she's used to finding only 3 percent to 5 percent that merit her time and the organization's expense for an interview.

With the odds stacked so heavily against resume writers, why would anyone decrease their chances by producing a document that gets hastily scanned and almost immediately banished forever to the reject pile? Why would anyone put blue jeans on a resume when they wouldn't dream of going to an interview wearing blue jeans? The resume gets the interview. It should be just as well dressed as you would be.

Improving Your Odds

If the odds are so bleak, you might conclude that any effort to improve them would be futile. Not so. In our experience—mine in developing a company that produced resumes for thousands of job seekers and Bill Fitzpatrick's in helping thousands of military people in their transitions to civilian life—we've seen the incredible success of job applicants who pay proper attention to their resumes. We've heard from plenty of successful job seekers who've used our approach in their job searches. They've reported back many times that interviewers granted interviews because they wanted to see the people who cared so much about themselves and their careers that they prepared and submitted first-class resumes.

There is one more dynamic at work here as well—there's more involved than caring for your career. You also need to exercise good judgment as an advertiser. For example, if you were writing an ad for your car, you would probably leave out that the car needed a paint job, or that it gets terrible gas mileage, or even that it needs new tires. You would dwell on the positive aspects of car ownership and list the positive features. The resume, of course, is no different. You are going to tell the potential employer only those things that will get her interested in talking to you. You are not going to include a list of items that say nothing about your ability to perform the job, such as height, weight, color of eyes, number of divorces, reasons for changing majors in college, or reasons why you didn't attend college or trade school. If you think you need a new paint job, don't point it out on your resume. You might just find that your qualifications and talents suit the employer just fine.

You've undoubtedly seen index cards advertising cars for sale by private owners—cards tacked to bulletin boards in supermarket lobbies, company lounges, wherever. And you've seen the kind with tons of words on them. You have to stand there and read the doggone thing, searching for the crucial information that it's a red Porsche 911 with 25,000 miles for just $12,000. Other index cards, however, stand out and invite your attention. Resumes, as you will learn, are no different. Remember, most people out there do as we used to do. They just whip their resumes together. They pay little attention to content. They have only the vaguest idea about what a resume is supposed to do. They employ the most tortured writing styles, produce busy and ineffective formats, and don't realize the importance of paper selection. That's your competition. It therefore makes sense for you to have a resume that stands out. One that grabs the attention of the employment manager when she first picks it up for that thirty-second review.

Getting to Know Your Consumer

Back to our employment manager. There she sits with her pile of resumes. From experience she knows she can get through the pile giving only thirty seconds to each one. Later she'll carefully read and study the let's-take-a-look pile. You've got thirty seconds of her time. Thirty seconds to make your pitch. And what else in life takes thirty seconds? That's right, a toothpaste commercial!

Before an ad agency produces a thirty-second TV commercial, what do you think it does first? Of course, the ad execs first brush their teeth with the client's toothpaste. "Tastes good," they say. "Whiter teeth, no doubt about that," they say. "Hmmm, fresher breath."

"But," they ask, "what does the consumer want?"

The ad execs conduct all kinds of studies and surveys to find out what prompts a typical consumer to conclude: "That's my brand. It has what I want!" They then prepare their thirty-second message to hammer home exactly how their brand delivers what the consumer wants.

The first task in preparing your resume, your thirty-second spot, is finding out what the consumer wants. You have already discovered in Chapter 1 those attributes the employment manager is looking for. Once you thoroughly understand what turns on the employment managers of this world, you must find evidence of these attributes in your life, in your education, in your personal qualities, in your work experience, in your travel, in your language ability, in your interests, and in your high school, college, community, or professional activities.

If the ad agency discovers the consumer wants whiter teeth and fresher breath, that's what the ad agency gives the consumer in the thirty-second ad. And now that you know the sixteen attributes the employment manager wants, that's what you will serve up in your thirty-second commercial . . . your resume.

How to Produce a Resume: Two Choices

Now that you understand some of the basics, let's talk about the mechanical aspects of putting together a first-class resume, one that will land you some solid interviews. There are two ways to produce a resume. You can write it yourself, or you can hire someone to write it for you. We have looked at both of these methods. Both leave something to be desired.

Realistically, resume writing is a very different writing style that even many experienced writers haven't developed. Even though you know more about yourself than anyone else does, and even though you may have some writing experience, the quality of the final resume that you write by yourself will be questionable. You could, however, hire someone to write your resume for you. That is going to cost you between fifty and two thousand dollars. For fifty dollars you will get a stack of resumes and some envelopes. For two thousand dollars you will get a stack of resumes and some envelopes . . . on nice paper. Most of the expensive ones will also include copies of a generic cover letter you can use to forward your resume to potential employers.

The quality of the work will vary, but high cost is not an indicator of a superior product. Generally, the companies that charge a particularly high fee also offer some other services such as help in developing a marketing plan, perhaps some personal training or coaching. Some will even put you in front of a video camera and let you see how silly you might look in an interview. We're not criticizing these companies, only trying to show you the range of services and fees. (Note: If some company tries to get you to sign a contract for services, be sure to read every line to ensure you know what you're getting. There are a lot of firms in the industry that lead you to believe they offer certain services, which they in fact do not.)

Resumes produced by commercial firms tend to look the same. In helping people in their career transitions, Bill Fitzpatrick reads 200–300 resumes each month. He often sees largely the same resume written for a salesperson with five years of service and a marketing director with over thirty years of experience in several fields. In the business world, resumes tend to look like everyone else's for a particular function and level. Some companies are very creative and really do an outstanding job. But how do you know who does good work and who copies from a generic template? You don't, so the results you will get from hiring a professional to write your resume are also questionable.

If you plan to hire a professional service, try to get a few names of previous customers. Then call those customers and find out how they felt about the services they received and how they fared in their searches for employment.

We feel the best way to produce a great resume is to combine these two methods. The first draft of the resume should be written by you, and then you can hire someone to polish your work. But throughout the entire process, you should maintain creative control. Don't just fill out a questionnaire and send it in with a check. You should stay involved and recommend not only the general direction of the resume but its format as well.

You provide the company with a reasonably complete draft, then they adjust and polish your draft.

So now you say, "Okay, I'll write it myself, but I still don't know anything about resumes." Read on!

The Perfect Resume

In preparing our lecture series and in researching material for the preparation of this book, we went in search of the perfect resume. We wanted to be able to create a blank form which would allow you to fill in the blocks and then produce a resume that would get you an interview every time. In our search we reviewed various authors and publications in detail. One source was fairly positive in stating that all resumes should appear exactly as he described. Another disagreed in favor of his particular version. A third cautioned against ever exceeding a single type-written sheet. A fourth, of course, urged two full pages. The last was certain that all resumes should be printed on light tan paper.

We were confused. Everyone claimed to be an expert and to have the only solution. They all disagreed. Our next step was to talk to various corporate executives who read resumes on a daily basis. They were very helpful. The first insisted that his favorite format would always cause him to want to talk to the individual described. Another insisted that the first recruiter was wrong and that her favorite version was much better in making selections. A third personnel professional felt anything over one page was too long to read, and a fourth really liked two-page resumes. The last participant in our study stated firmly that the best resumes were printed on (you guessed it) light tan paper.

What a dilemma. We were now more confused than ever. And then it finally came to us . . . . There is no perfect resume. The best resume is the one that best displays your qualifications. Everyone is different, and every industry seeks different qualifications, so each of the authors and each of the executives we talked to was right. Their choices of resumes were based on the kinds of people they were seeking or describing.

You are in the same situation. Determining the right kind of resume, with the best format and the best paper, is going to be influenced by your qualifications and the real needs of the marketplace, not by your personal interests and desires nor by the standards of experts. A resume company should never use the same approach for every client because each one is unique. Why would you select a resume that emphasizes education when you have only a high school GED? Why would you use a resume that places education at the bottom of the second page, buried in the middle of a paragraph, when you have a doctorate? Why would you want to select a chronologically organized resume when you've had a break in employment, plus time away to serve in the Army Reserve, when the resume gives the impression that you were unemployable for some period?

Everyone is different. Therefore you have to spend some time doing your own research to determine which kind of resume best suits your qualifications. Then you will have a good starting point from which to write that important first draft, hire a professional to polish your work, and get your own personal advertisement out there in the marketplace working for you.

Types of Resumes

Basically, there are three kinds of resumes: the chronological resume, the functional resume, and the combination resume. After working with many executives in their job searches, we developed a new type of resume especially useful for professionals and managers. So to the basic three types of resumes we've added a fourth variation: the functional subheading resume. The chronological resume categorizes your life in chronological order, from the most recent event back in time within each category. The functional resume, on the other hand, describes your abilities or competencies without regard to category of experience or to the chronology of events. The combination resume adopts the chronological approach for most of your life but includes a functional-like description of your strongest points. The functional subheading resume adopts a chronological format but uses functional subheadings to draw together particular traits the employer is looking for. To help you decide which resume is right for you, let's review each one separately.

Chronological Resume

The chronological resume shows your education, employment, activities, and other information about you in chronological order with the most recent event under each heading listed first. The entries in the chronological resume will be employers, colleges, groups, organizations, clubs, and teams. The content of each entry describes what you did, when you did it, and what you accomplished. Naturally, you will write each entry with the consumer in mind: you'll describe your experiences in a way that proves you've got what it takes to do the job and do it well.

The chronological resume is the most common type, and most employers prefer it. On the plus side, it enables you to highlight the jobs you have had, the organizations you have been affiliated with, the positions of leadership you have held. It lets the employer track your career, to see evidence of advancement, to see diversity, to see accomplishments. Employers like the chronological resume because it enables them to make their own conclusions about your attributes, your competencies, your abilities.

On the negative side the chronological resume may emphasize the outward facts of your experience—which may not look impressive—at the expense of your real strengths. For example, the chronological resume makes it difficult for you to hide gaps in your employment. For a graduating student, this could mean the summer you spent relaxing by the pool contemplating the origins of the universe. For a professional, this might be the year or two you took off from the firm to write a novel or try a new business venture. For women reentering the workforce, the chronological resume makes it difficult to track a scattered employment history under the traditional Employment heading. In the chronological resume it's hard to conceal what you think are distinctly unexciting jobs, or jobs that you had to take that were far off your career track. Finally, the chronological resume makes it difficult to reveal true abilities you do have that don't show up very well in a chrono- logical listing of experiences; sometimes if you simply reveal your experience from the most recent assignment back in time, it's difficult to bring similar skills or abilities, gained at different times, together in one place on the resume.

Functional Resume

The functional resume is entirely different. Instead of listing the companies you've worked for or positions you've had, the functional resume describes your competencies or abilities as represented by your jobs, activities, athletics, travel, or whatever.

To illustrate, suppose in your career, you've gained signifi- cant experience as a personnel recruiter, through a number of different assignments within the same corporation. If you chose a chronological resume, you would be detailing each position or assignment you had, and slowly but surely the resume reviewer would get a picture of your experience in the field of human resources. A functional resume would expedite this pro- cess by bringing the relevant experience and ability together into one resume entry. It might look like this:

> Human Resources Experience: Positions of increasing scope and responsi- bility within the personnel department of Super Micro, Inc., in several major markets across the United States. Experience began with the posi- tion of personnel interviewer and culminated as the Special Assistant to the Vice President for Personnel, responsible for all hiring activities nationally for three corporate divisions, entailing the hiring of over 1,500 employees annually for Super Micro.

Suppose you're a graduating student with a lot of entre- preneurial talent, a talent you confirmed when you saw a recur- ring entrepreneurial pattern on your Pay, Free, and Like-to-Do pages. On your Pay page you wrote that you ran a lemonade stand at age six, which grossed $350 in only three weeks. (That was a long time ago, but you think it's significant.) Also on your Pay page you recalled the birthday cake delivery service you ran during your sophomore year in college. On your Free page you wrote down that project you dreamed up for the high school football team to sell advertising space in the football programs. You also made note of the rock concerts you successfully organized to raise money for your fraternity. And on the Like-to-Do page you wrote, "Enjoy dreaming up new ideas and putting them into action to earn money." If you choose a chronological resume, then where and how is this entrepreneurial talent of yours going to be revealed? The lemonade stand probably should be under Employment; if it is, it'll be the last entry in the chronological format. Perhaps you'd decide to create a special heading called Early Background or Personal Background in which you would reveal your entrepreneurial conquests as a child. The birthday cake delivery service? You'd probably put that under Employment along with those ho-hum jobs you had to take back home to earn enough money to return to college the next year. The high school football project? That would probably come under Activities or perhaps Athletics. The rock concerts? They would probably come under Activities as well. You can see that your very real ability in entrepreneurship is scattered among several different headings in the chronological resume.

The functional resume, on the other hand, allows you to lump all these events in your life under one heading as follows:

Entrepreneurial Ability:	Ran successful lemonade stand at age six, which grossed $350 in only three weeks; launched moneymaking series of rock concerts for fraternity in senior year of college; started and successfully operated a birthday cake delivery service in sophomore year, which paid for more than 50% of college costs; instituted for the first time the sale of advertising space in high school football program resulting in gross revenues of $2,500 during the first year of operation.

You can readily see that the functional resume can be a very effective tool. It can convey abilities that will spark an employer's interest. But a word of caution: employers don't like the functional resume. They'd rather make their own conclusions about your abilities or competencies. We think employers are correct in their dislike of the functional resume for one important reason: resume writers too often incorrectly choose it. They've seen some sample functional resumes and try to plug their lives into them when their lives just don't fit. They list a super-impressive heading such as Leadership Ability and then fill it with weak information.

Resume writers incorrectly choose the functional resume because they conclude they have to use certain headings, which don't really pertain to their ability or experience. They incorrectly think every resume must have the broad heading Demonstrated Skills or Competencies. They then proceed to put in the subheadings of the sample resume they're cribbing. (Yeah, we know you do it, and we'll have a word about that later.) Then they try to squeeze their lives into the copied format. Here's what they end up with:

DEMONSTRATED SKILLS:

Leadership:	Served on Alumni Day Committee of college sorority. Volunteered to help with fundraising projects of high school service club.
Writing Skills:	Wrote two term papers for college history course.
Interpersonal Skills:	During high school employment and college summer employment, worked directly with customers at a fashion boutique. Also served as a Big Sister for a disadvantaged child during college.

This resume reveals somebody trying to say she has exhibited leadership qualities when she hasn't. She's trying to show writing experience when she has very little. It turns out that she does have good interpersonal skills, which she developed at the fashion boutique. But this person also held that fashion boutique job for four straight summers, was given increases in pay each summer, took over management of the office during the owner's absence, and worked more than fifty hours a week during the summers and twenty hours a week during high school academic years. Her remarkable energy level message was completely lost because she was trying to squeeze her life into another person's functional resume.

Follow these rules in deciding whether to use the functional resume: (1) be sure that you and not somebody else chooses the headings; (2) make certain you really possess strong evidence of the attributes described by those headings; (3) be certain the functional resume is the only way you can reveal your qualities; and (4) make sure these qualities appear on all of your self-assessment pages, or at least on the Pay, Free, and Like-to-Do pages. If a quality doesn't appear on these three pages, chances are it isn't that pervasive in your life.

Another word of caution on the functional resume: Many resume-writing services will use a functional format for their resumes. Mistake number one. Then they'll use the third person in writing the resume, making it sound as if it is talking about somebody else. Here's what you'll find:

DEMONSTRATED LEADERSHIP:
Takes charge of the Quality Control Department of a large manufacturing concern with direct responsibility over Quality Control Supervisors. Delegates authority. Controls annual budget. Demonstrates leadership abilities in all facets of professional responsibility.

Ugh. First of all, employers want to read your writing about yourself, not some piece that sounds like a cheap biography. Second, employers would rather see who you worked for, when you did it, what you accomplished, and how you advanced.

In many cases, your best bet is to use a chronological format but incorporate the advantages of the functional resume by using either the combination or the functional subheading resume.

Combination Resume

The combination resume is a chronological resume with one or two functional headings or sub-headings. In other words, you follow a chronological format for Education, Employment, and perhaps Activities. But one of your abilities is really strong, so you drive home this point under a functional heading, like the previous Entrepreneurial Ability example. Or you worked a long time in one place where your responsibilities were unusually varied. The pattern of your development there might get lost in the chronology, so for that entry you use some functional subheadings to bring together your strongest areas of experience from that period, as in the previous Human Resources Experience example. Of course, if you use this approach across the board, you produce the fourth resume type.

Functional Subheading Resume

We've used the functional subheading resume successfully with many executives engaged in highly competitive job searches. It uses a chronological format but incorporates functional subheadings within the Employment heading to drive home the strengths of the candidate or the attributes sought by the employer. Though we'll return to this type of resume later, here, briefly, is how it works.

Suppose you've worked for the same company for fifteen years. You've held various positions at various locations around the country, and steadily climbed up the ladder. In a pure chronological resume, you'd portray each position held chronologically back in time. The trouble is, when you take that approach, you find yourself saying the same things about yourself over and over again. Instead of adopting this pure chronological approach, you elaborate on your chronological entries with functional subheadings.

Suppose you're a computer systems manager for a mid-sized company. You got where you are by steadily advancing within the company at various locations. You've held a variety of positions ranging from an entry-level computer operator, to programmer, to assistant manager, to computer systems manager. Analyzing your market, you determine that your prospective employers are looking for computer experience, a working knowledge of hardware and software, managerial capability, and the ability to control costs.

Instead of portraying your work experience chronologically, here's what you do:

Computer Management:	***ACME Consulting Associates,*** Washington, DC **Computer Systems Manager,** 1988–present. Began in 1975 as a Computer Operator with this large consulting firm with nationwide operations. Held various positions throughout the country, steadily advancing to current managerial post. Gained significant experience in the field of computer systems management:

- ***Experience with Computers.*** Worked with a variety of microcomputer systems including IBMs and DECs. Recently supervised the installation of a 50-PC network for financial analysts consisting of shared software, printers, electronic mail, computerized billing, consulting scheduling, word processing, and desktop publishing.
- ***Managerial Experience.*** Currently recruit, hire, train, and supervise a staff of 25 computer operators serving a 50-member staff of financial consultants.
- ***Budgetary Control.*** Charged with controlling costs within a stringent and carefully prepared annual budget. Consistently stay within budget. Most recently, instituted a "materials cost-cutting program" that reduced annual supply costs by more than $10,000.

Which Resume Is Right for You?

The majority of people should use the chronological resume because employers prefer it. Rarely, if ever, should you use a strictly functional resume. Few people are extremely strong in a sufficient number of categories or headings to fill up a functional resume. Of course, if you have extremely good experiences that demonstrate a highly desirable attribute, and those experiences would be scattered in a chronological resume, you should use the combination resume and include a heading that appropriately describes this strength.

Resume choice is often dictated by your current status. The following chart should prove useful in choosing the type of resume best for you.

CHOOSING A RESUME TYPE

Job Searcher	Resume Type
Professionals/managers	
Age 20–30	Chronological or Combination
Age 30 and up	Chronological or Functional Subheading
College student	Chronological or Combination
Homemaker reentering the workforce	Chronological (with carefully selected headings, see Chapter 4), Functional Subheading
High school student	Chronological (with carefully selected headings, see Chapter 4)

Resume Structure

Now that you have some idea about resume types, it's time to get down to the nuts and bolts. Let's look at the basic structure of resumes so you can begin to get your job search ready for launching.

We're now going to review the parts of a resume: caption, objective, headings, entries, leads, and dates.

Caption

All resumes should begin with a caption revealing your name, address, and telephone number. Your name should be your formal name. If it's James Frederick McAllister and you go by Fred, then your name should appear as J. Frederick McAllister. Don't include your nickname; employers can learn that in the interview. Generally your name should be centered at the top of your resume, although some people effectively put it flush to the far left margin. Try to accentuate your name by putting it in capital letters or in bold type. Finally, you should not put the word *Resume* at the top of your resume. Employers know what they're reading.

If you've centered your name, then center your address under your name. Or if you've put your name to the far left margin, put your address and telephone number directly under your name.

Thus, your caption might appear as either of the following:

J. FREDERICK McALLISTER
301 Gentry Lane
Baltimore, MD 32122
(301) 442-4444

J. FREDERICK McALLISTER
301 Gentry Lane
Baltimore, MD 32122
(301) 442-4444

Two-Address Caption.   If you are currently in college or graduate school and are not residing at home, then you should include two addresses. You can call one your School Address, Current Address, or Present Address. The other you can call your Home Address or Permanent Address. You want to include both in case the employer wants to invite you for an interview during a vacation or break and can't reach you at your school address. Your telephone numbers at school and at home should appear as the last bit of information in the respective addresses. Thus, your two-address caption should appear as follows:

J. FREDERICK McALLISTER

School Address:	Home Address:
34 Cabell Avenue, N.W.	301 Gentry Lane
Charlottesville, VA 22901	Baltimore, MD 32122
(804) 999-8989	(301) 442-4444

Office Address.   Finally, if you're currently working for a company and putting a resume together in order to find a better, higher-paying position, you've got to be careful about using a caption with both home and work addresses or with both home and work telephone numbers. If you currently work for an impressive company, there are some good arguments that you should include an office address. The question boils down to whether you want your current employer's receptionist to receive telephone calls from your prospective employers. Sometimes it's good for your current employers to know you're looking around. Suddenly they'll see your value and offer you a raise. But if you feel uncomfortable, you should probably exclude your office address and office telephone number. Instead, give out this information in your cover letters and request employers to contact you in confidence.

Objective

Many career advisors describe this section as optional, but we feel it is critical to the success of the document. If you write a good career objective and then write the resume to support the objective you will stay focused on accomplishments that support your capabilities. This section has many titles, such as Career Objective, Career Goal, Professional Objective, Professional Goal, or simply Objective or Goal. The title is not important, but the content is. The rule here is twofold: first, stay focused on a single objective; second, don't tell employers what you expect from them, but tell them what you are going to do for their companies.

A Note for Students and for People "Looking Around."   Before you even try to write a job objective, you should first decide whether you really have one. Many college students and most high school students, for example, don't really know what they want to do. Many don't even know what there is to do in this world. Let's face it, colleges and high schools don't exactly teach you what you can do with your life. So it's likely many students won't have a precise idea of what they want to do. Similarly, many people just starting out in the work world may not know yet what direction they want to pursue, and some people with a great deal of work experience may be looking for a change without having a clear idea of what that change might be. The answer for you is simple: do not include an objective on your resume! The last thing you want to do is write a terribly soupy objective, like this one:

> Objective: To obtain an exciting and challenging position enabling me to apply my organizational and interpersonal skills.

That objective shows no direction at all. To have a true job objective you should be able to answer two and perhaps three questions: (1) What kind of position do I seek? (2) What kind of company or organization do I want to work for? (3) Where in the United States or the world do I want to live? If you really do have an objective that is position-specific, industry- or organization-specific, and perhaps location-specific, then you should write a job objective.

For instance, if you want to work in public relations or advertising with a large company in the Northeast, then your objective can say:

> Objective: An advertising or public relations position with a large company in the Northeast.

We remember talking with a college senior who wanted to go into investment banking on Wall Street. He had written a host of possible objectives. We quizzed him extensively about investment bankers. We all agreed they were not the type of people who would be thrilled about an applicant who seeks "an exciting position that will utilize my interpersonal skills and extensive background in finance." We agreed that investment bankers are probably a pretty conservative bunch. So here's the terse objective we devised.

> Objective: Investment Banking.

What's-in-It-for-Me.   Here are some examples of what we like to call what's-in-it-for-me objectives:

Objective: A challenging management position in a results-oriented company where I can rise to my full potential.

Objective: An upwardly mobile position in a major corporation where people are regarded as assets.

Objective: A position in sales or management where advancement is according to published guidelines.

Objective: A position in management.

Objective: A position in management with a forward-thinking organization where there is room for personal and professional growth.

Objective: To obtain an entry-level position in a management training program that will utilize my skills in management, finance, and accounting, and will offer professional rewards.

Obviously the authors of these objectives are sending an interesting message to a future employer. Although all of these objectives describe situations any of us would like to find, the employer is going to get the impression that the job seeker is very self-oriented.

A better approach would be to focus on the industry and then tell the company what you will do for them. Thus, when you write your objective, think of how the employer will benefit from hiring you, and then say that. One effective way, of course, is to use the verb *benefit*. If you're just starting out, it may be enough to show your desire for an entry-level position. Some examples of this method:

Objective: An entry-level position in Human Resources Management.

Objective: An entry-level position in a management training program with a company that will benefit from my highly developed organizational skills and solid background in finance.

Objective: To work with a commercial bank in the Sun Belt that will benefit from my extensive background in Accounting, my proven desire to produce consistently good work, and my insistence on professionalism.

Objective: An opportunity to apply 20+ years of leadership and management experience to company objectives in the field of industrial management.

Objective: A position in Quality Assurance where upward mobility is based on demonstrated performance.

Objective: A position in financial management.

Objective: A position in sales (or sales management) where income is based upon performance.

Those objectives stand a better chance of making the employment manager want to meet the people who wrote them. And, indeed, that's the purpose of a resume: to get an interview.

One of these days maybe we will see the truly honest job objective. Somebody out there please try this one and let us know how it works!

Objective: To make a bunch of money. For my company. And for me.

Multiple Objectives. Sometimes an objective can cramp your style. After all, if you have an objective that says, "To obtain a management position with a large commercial bank in the Northeast," you'd have a hard time submitting that resume to get a terrific job that opens up with Delta Airlines in Atlanta. Also, people often haven't really narrowed their chosen careers to a particular position with a particular industry in a particular part of the country. In fact, a resume writer might want a job on the East Coast but be perfectly happy with the same type of job on the West Coast.

To give yourself flexibility, you can easily have one set resume with multiple objectives. That is, you really have two or more resumes, each bearing a different objective. If you have a personal computer or access to one, you should electronically store your resume. By having a set resume stored on your computer, you can easily change job objectives or other resume information. In short, you can tailor your resume, especially the job objective, to fit the position you seek with a particular company.

A Personal Profile

If you've decided a job objective is not for you, you might consider using a personal profile or summary of qualifications as a substitute. This technique was recently recommended by the *National Business Employment Weekly*, published by the *Wall Street Journal*. As the first heading of your resume, this personal profile can immediately grab an employer's attention and in a couple of sentences make a strong case for your resume to end up in the let's-take-a-look pile.

To write this section effectively you must toss all remnants of humility out the window, take a deep breath, and proceed to congratulate yourself. The personal profile should consume just one or two sentences, drive home your strongest talents, and verify these talents by specifically referring to the strongest experience you've had. Here are samples for a forty-year-old sales manager, a homemaker reentering the job market, a college student, and a graduating high school student.

Forty-Year-Old Sales Manager

Personal Profile: Sales Manager with (1) 15 years experience in direct sales, telemarketing, direct mail marketing, and sales management; (2) a consistent record of exceeding sales quotas; (3) the proven ability to motivate a sales staff; and (4) the competitive desire to grow with an aggressive company.

Homemaker Reentering the Job Market

Personal Profile: Energetic, highly organized, and ambitious individual who, while simultaneously raising three children, gained valuable experience in budgeting, finance, management, motivation, and organization as Director of Fundraising for the local rescue squad.

College Student

Personal   Extremely hard-working individual who earned 50%
Profile: of college costs working 15 hours per week during
school while earning a 3.4 GPA in major. Extensive
writing experience gained through writing a host
of term papers and one major thesis.

High School Student

Personal   Conscientious high school student who held part-time
Profile: jobs throughout the academic year, participated in
two varsity sports, and maintained a solid "B" average.
Gained significant work experience dealing directly
with the public.

These personal profiles communicate many attributes
employers are seeking: energy level, intelligence, communication skills, competition, leadership, goal achievement, and
others. But the profile doesn't just assert these things. It demonstrates the qualities by specifically referring to evidence of the
attributes in the person's background and accomplishments.

By having this personal profile you produce many of the
results created by a job objective: you grab the employer's
attention, toot your horn, and make him want to read on. Yet
you don't hem yourself in as you might with a job objective.

Caption and Objective: A Summary

Every resume regardless of type will begin with a caption. Then
some resumes will follow with the objective or personal profile.
Other resumes will have no objective and no personal profile. They will just begin with the appropriate heading immediately following the caption. An example of a proper caption
and objective appears below:

J. FREDERICK McALLISTER
301 Gentry Lane
Baltimore, MD 32122
(301) 442-4444

Objective: To obtain a position in sales with a chemical manufacturing company in the Southeast that will benefit from my substantial sales experience and that will provide suitable financial incentives to reward top performance.

Headings, Entries, Leads, and Dates

Let's define some terms so you can understand the structure of your resume. Your resume will be divided into headings such as Education, Employment, Activities, and others (a fairly complete list of potential headings appears below). Within each heading will appear several entries, which describe an educational degree, a job, an activity, and so on. Each entry will begin with a lead, which you can use very effectively to direct the employment manager's attention to your strongest experience. Also within an entry, you might have some functional subheadings to draw together the types of experience and ability you've gained. And finally, a date will appear, with some entries, to state when you held a particular job or received a particular degree. Let's look at two examples of the use of these terms:

Education: **University of Virginia,** Charlottesville, VA
B.A. in History, May 1991. Broad liberal arts curriculum required extensive writing. Completed a 50-page paper surveying the role of biography in historical analysis. GPA in Major = 3.3.

In the above example the word Education is a heading. The entire block of information that follows is an entry. The words University of Virginia constitute the lead. And, obviously, May 1991 is the date.

Employment: **Super Micro, Inc.,** Kansas City, MO
Completed a 15-year career with this major computer manufacturer, beginning as a personnel recruiter. Advanced through a host of assignments, primarily in the field of personnel. 1975–1990.

Gained experience as a midlevel manager in the following areas:

- **Human Resources.** Positions of increasing scope and responsibility within the personnel department in several major markets across the United States. Experience began with the position of personnel recruiter and culminated as the Special Assistant to the Vice President for Personnel, responsible for all hiring activities for Super Micro's midwestern offices and facilities.
- **Personnel Management.** Supervised a staff of six other personnel managers, four clerical persons, and various part-time employees.
- **Team-Building.** Instilled a sense of teamwork among subordinates, resulting in a 30% increase in the efficiency of hiring at the Kansas City headquarters.

In the above example, the word *Employment* is the heading. The words *Super Micro, Inc.* are the lead. The paragraphs describing the experience are the entry. The words *1975–1990* are obviously the date. And the bulleted words *Human Resources, Personnel Management,* and *Team-Building* are functional subheadings enabling you to draw your abilities together in one place.

In this chapter we're concerned only with learning the structure of a resume. In the next chapter on resume content we'll see how you can manipulate these ingredients to accomplish your mission of selling yourself in thirty seconds flat.

Potential Headings in a Chronological Resume. Although we'll discuss each of these headings in detail in the next chapter, here are some potential headings that might appear in a chronological resume:

Education   Employment   Community Service
Experience   Travel   Publications

Activities	Languages	Interests
Honors	Awards	Personal
Athletics	References	Military Service

This is not a rigid list. Indeed, there's plenty of room for creativity in writing your resume. For example, maybe you've volunteered to do a lot of political work and the Community Service heading just doesn't fit. Instead, you may use Political Work, Political Activity, or some other appropriate heading.

Modifying Headings.   You can also modify headings with other words. For example, maybe you're going after a position in personnel and have the word *personnel* in your objective. Then to show the experience you have in personnel, you ignore the Employment heading and use Personnel Experience instead. You can readily see how modified headings can target your resume to the precise consumer you want.

Here's just a small sampling of creative headings produced by the modification technique:

Computer Experience	Writing Experience
Sales Experience	Retail Experience
Financial Experience	Banking Experience
Summer Employment	School Employment
Political Activities	Foreign Travel
Sales Management	Experience in Persuasion

The list of modified headings could go on and on. For now, just keep in mind that *you* are in charge of selecting or creating headings that package you and your life most persuasively and effectively. In the next chapter we'll see how you can position or sequence information in your resume by intentionally creating headings that pertain specifically to your background or to your overall career goals.

Sample Headings in a Functional Resume.   Here's a list of potential headings you might use in a functional or indeed a combination resume.

Demonstrated Skills	Competencies
Leadership Ability	Communication Skills
Organizational Ability	Writing Ability
Managerial Capacity	Motivational Skills
Interpersonal Skills	Athletic Ability

We should caution you once again to take great care in devising headings for the functional resume. Be sure you dream up the headings. Make absolutely certain you can show strong credentials and experiences in each functional heading. Never, ever copy the functional headings from another person's resume.

Sample Subheadings in a Functional Subheading Resume. Recall that functional subheadings provide an excellent way to organize an entire professional career. The list of potential subheadings, of course, is endless. But here is a starter list to help you analyze your own background and come up with your own:

Budget Control	Personnel Management
Managerial Ability	Marketing Ability
Computer Graphics	Writing Ability
Quality Control	Recruitment
Sales Meetings	Motivation of Staff
Team-building	

Now comes the fun part—writing your resume.

CHAPTER 4

What Goes Where

Inside Your Resume

YOU'LL NOW BEGIN TO review your experience to decide what to include in your resume. As you do this, keep several things in mind. First, don't include every bit of information about yourself. If you do, you'll end up with an inordinately long resume that will bore employers to tears. Second, if you're a high school student or college student, try to get your resume on one page. If you're over thirty, you probably need a two-page resume. Try to avoid a three-page resume, and never go beyond three pages.

Third, in deciding what to include, apply the does-it-help? test. Look at each bit of information and ask, "Does it help my message?" If the answer is no, then the information stays off. For instance, if your GPA was 1.8 or even 2.8, that information stays off your resume. Unless you're a graduating high school student, look hard at that high school activity you're dying to include on your resume and ask yourself, "If the employer knows this about me, will I get an interview?" The honest answer to many of these questions will be, "Nope, it just doesn't help one way or the other." If you *are* a high school student, of course, that activity might very well be the focus of much of your resume.

Overview

Having taken a quick look at the rules dictating the overall content and length of your resume, in this chapter we're going to review each potential heading in a chronological resume to see what might appear in each heading. We'll then talk about the strategy you should use to position your headings in the proper sequence. Following that we'll discuss the all-important technique of choosing the right leads. And finally, we're going to clear up the horrible mistakes people make with the dates on their resumes.

Visiting the Various Headings

Let's begin a detailed review of the potential headings of a chronological resume and see what kind of information should appear in each. By the time you finish studying this section, you should have a good idea about which headings should appear in your resume.

Here's a review of the headings, in no particular order.

Education

The Education heading is perhaps the most important for those who are under thirty. After all, educational endeavors consume (or should consume) the college and graduate student. Your college experience, coursework, and college activities might constitute the strongest part of your background.

Over-thirty readers are likely to find the importance of their educational backgrounds pales in comparison to their professional experiences. Does an employment manager really care about the educational background and achievements of a forty-five-year-old sales manager? No, the employment manager wants to know if the sales manager can sell widgets. In the professions, however, academic prowess can still be important long after the diploma has slipped a little in its gilded frame. The relative importance of educational background, of course, will determine both the positioning and prominence of the Education heading.

Within the Education heading, your first entry should be your most recent educational experience, which is probably your college or graduate school. The entry should include the name of your college, the city and state where the college is, the degree you received or expect to receive, and the date of the degree. You need not include the mailing address of the college or institution.

Those under thirty might want to consider beefing up the Education heading by including some mention of curriculum, honors and awards, and GPA—all dealt with below. The over-thirty crowd probably should just list the college or university, the city and state, the degree received, and the date.

Curriculum. College and graduate students should keep in mind that employers are looking for intelligence, direction, vocational skills, career preparation, and communication ability. Thus, you might include a brief description of your curriculum and academic experience that relate directly to the type of employment you seek. For instance, if you're seeking a banking position, don't say your curriculum included several courses in Marxist-Leninist thought, Russian history, and Third World exploitation. Instead, pick out your business-related courses and say your curriculum included micro- and macroeconomics, money and banking, accounting, marketing, and finance.

If you're going after computer jobs, list your most significant computer courses, your programming languages, major software programs you've mastered, and perhaps the type of hardware you've operated as part of your course experience. If you've had writing experience, emphasize your writing ability. You can even name the major papers you wrote if they relate directly to the type of employment you seek. If you've had speech courses or courses requiring oral presentations, describe these briefly. If you participated in the debate club, you can include that under your college entry in the Education heading. Or, if this experience is particularly strong, you might pull it out and put it in a separate heading called Public Speaking Experience. Remembering your audience, review the attributes they're looking for, find these attributes in yourself, and serve them up.

Honors and Awards as a Subheading of Education.   College and graduate students, if you have some academic honors and awards, you might choose to put them under the Education heading. You might even have a subheading called Honors and Awards, which lists the honors and awards you received. On the other hand, if you're particularly strong in the honors and awards area, you might correctly choose to put them in their own separate heading, equally prominent with Education, Employment, and your other headings. (We discuss this option in detail beginning on page 78.)

GPA Problems.   Finally, you might want to include your GPA. "What?" you scream. "You mean I've gotta put my grades in this thing?" Well, maybe and maybe not. Let's pause for a moment and deal with what we might call the GPA Problem.

As with all resume information, you include only information that helps you. A good cutoff for GPA is the magic number 3.0. So if you've got a 3.0, then include it. You can't quite squeeze out a 3.0? Well, try this. How about your major? Do you have a 3.0 in your major? If so, then write, "GPA in Major = 3.0." Can't quite make a 3.0 out of your grades in your major courses? Well, how about during the last two years? No? How about in the last year? There's absolutely nothing wrong with writing, "GPA during last academic year = 3.0."

When you reveal your GPA, it's often helpful to show the grading scale at your college or university. This is especially true if your college doesn't use the 4.0 scale, or if potential employers are not familiar with your institution. If so, indicate your GPA this way: "GPA = 3.2 on a 4.0 scale."

Alternative to GPA.   If you can't even squeeze out a 3.0 in the last course you took, leave your GPA out altogether. Don't even mention it. But you might take a hard look at yourself and see if there were any reasons why you didn't reach the magic number.

Did you work your way through school? Well, then, write this: "Worked 20 hours per week during school to earn 100% of education costs while carrying a full academic load."

The need to put your GPA in the best light or find a good alternative is probably most critical for graduating students participating in on-campus recruiting. At many universities students must agree to permit the placement office to give out their GPAs on request to employers. Even though GPA usually isn't important in getting a job, it's often an easy way for employment managers facing a stack of 300 resumes to decide whom they'll interview on campus.

Test Scores. If your GPA isn't all that thrilling, perhaps you have good SAT scores. If so, then list them: SAT = 580 Verbal, 620 Math. If you're currently in law school, business school, medical school, or some other graduate program, you might also list your LSAT, GRE, MCAT, or any other academic score. If you're not certain prospective employers will understand the significance of a raw number, then include your score as a percentile. For example, we consulted with an extremely bright and capable young woman in Charlottesville who was about to receive her Ph.D. in Biology. She had decided to remain in Charlottesville, where the demand for Ph.D's isn't great. So we created two resumes for her, her townie resume and her academic resume. In the townie resume we wrote this: "Scored in the 99th percentile on the Analytical Ability portion of the Graduate Record Exams." On the academic resume we listed each score, figuring that those receiving this resume would know the significance of the numbers.

What About High School? A perennially tough question is, "What about high school?" Should your high school be listed on your resume? The answer, like most, is maybe yes and maybe no. If you're a professional who has a hard time remembering the year of your high school graduation, then you should banish high school from your resume. It eats up too much precious room and undoubtedly flunks the does-it-help? test.

If you are currently or were recently in graduate school or college, you might very well include your high school in any one of the following three situations: (1) the school is well known, such as Exeter, Choate, the Madeira School, or a school held in high regard in the area where you're looking for employment; (2) you held a significant office or received an impressive award in high school; or (3) you are applying for employment in your hometown, and you want to show your provincialism, your roots. If none of these situations applies, however, it's time to kiss high school goodbye! If you do include high school, be careful. Perhaps you were extraordinarily active in high school but not so active in college. A large, impressive high school entry juxtaposed with a short, skimpy college entry doesn't exactly show you're on the upswing. So restrict your high school entry to your two or three outstanding accomplishments.

High school students, of course, will feature their high school, their high school activities, and all other positive activities they've been pursuing.

What If I Didn't Finish College?   Many resume writers didn't finish college. Perhaps you completed a couple of years, ran out of money, found a job with the intention of returning to college, liked the job, and just never returned. Do you include the Education heading on your resume. Yes, but you don't give it much play. If you've got a two-page resume, position the Education heading somewhere on the second page. Then your incomplete college career might appear as follows:

Education: **Stoney Creek Community College**, Pineville, NC
Completed two years of General Business courses including Accounting, Finance, Budgeting, Sales, and Management. 1971–73.

Continuing Education or On-the-Job Training.   Many people have so-so college backgrounds but outstanding continuing or employment educational experiences. If you count yourself in this group, you've got the chance to score some points while downplaying your so-so college experience. First, you should divide your educational experience into two headings, one called

Education and one called Professional Training (or Sales Training, Management Training, Computer Training, or whatever). Position the job-training heading on page one and the Education heading on page two. In the professional training heading, simply describe the name of the course, its duration, and its curriculum. Like this:

Professional   <u>XEROX SALES TRAINING PROGRAM</u>
Training: Completed the highly regarded Xerox sales
                training course, an intensive program covering
                all facets of sales: prospecting, records manage-
                ment, presentations, closes, follow-up, and goal
                achievement. Fall 1991.

Some Examples of the Education Heading.   Before we move on to the Honors and Awards heading, let's pause and look at some sample Education headings and the entries, leads, and dates that might appear within them.

In the first example we have a student whose credentials speak for themselves. She was extremely active in college, and her summer jobs are singularly impressive. Because her activities and employment show her energy level, vocational skills, and ability to communicate, she includes no description of her curriculum and lets her college experience loudly shout: intelligence. She needs to reduce the size of the Education heading to save space for other headings. She just lets her academic accomplishments tell their own story. Here's how she pulls it off:

Education: <u>Yale University</u>, New Haven, Connecticut
            B.A. in International Relations, June 1991.
            Magna Cum Laude. Cumulative GPA = 3.75 on a
            4.0 scale.

In the next example we have a student with a so-so academic performance, no college activities, and distinctly unexciting summer jobs. He needs to fill up some space and hammer home the message that he has the requisite energy level and vocational skills for a computer job.

Education: **B.S. in Computer Science,** Pine Stump Tech, Mapp, Ohio. Degree expected in June of 1991. Worked 20 hours per week while taking a full courseload and full-time during the summers to pay for 75% of all college costs. Curriculum included extensive programming in D-Base. Senior project entailed designing, programming, and testing a billing system for a small law office.

Honors and Awards

Resumes often include a heading called "Honors and Awards." As mentioned above, some people will effectively place this information as a subheading under the educational institution where the honor or award was earned. This technique eliminates the need to explain the source or location of the honor or award. Other people, of course, effectively display their honors and awards in a separate heading.

When writing this section, assume your audience is completely ignorant. They undoubtedly are ignorant of the names and significance of the overwhelming majority of honors and awards given in the United States. They don't have the foggiest notion that the Raven Society at the University of Virginia recognizes outstanding leadership and contributions to the University. It could just as well be a bird-watching club. Of course, some awards are self-explanatory or so well known they don't need any explanation. Everybody knows about the National Honor Society in high school. Certainly recruiters will recognize the value of National Merit Finalist. But for most awards or honors some explanation of purpose and selectivity is definitely needed.

As you list your honors and awards, include a brief description of their significance. If you were one of only two from a high school, an entire city, or an entire state to receive an award, then you should show this high selectivity of the award. Or if you received an honor or award given only to a small percentage of an entire group, then also show selectivity. On the other hand, if you were one of fifty in a class of one hundred to receive an award, naturally don't breathe a word about how easy it was to receive it.

The following two examples show how the Honors and Awards section should be written. Notice how the awards are briefly explained if their names don't reveal their purpose. In example 1 the student has decided to include Honors and Awards as a subheading in the Education heading. In example 2 Honors and Awards is included as a separate heading.

Example 1

Education: **University of Ames**, Ames, Washington. B.A. in History, May 1991. GPA in Major = 3.4. Curriculum required extensive writing, including a Senior Thesis studying governmental regulation of business in the 1920s. Political science courses included The Political Parties of the United States, Presidential Elections, American Judicial Process, and Constitutional Law.

Honors & Awards: The President's Trophy (awarded to the two seniors in class of 350 who made outstanding contributions to university life).

Ames Lions Club Scholarship ($1,000 scholarship awarded to one graduating high school senior from the city of Ames).

Example 2

Honors & Awards: **Sheldon Gray Memorial Citizenship Award** (presented to the high school graduating senior in the state of Tennessee displaying high attributes of good citizenship).

Dean's List (five out of six semesters).

Valedictorian of high school class of 650 students.

In the above examples the President's Trophy, Ames Lions Club Scholarship, and Sheldon awards were explained because nobody knows what they represent. The Dean's List honor is commonly known, but since the student made the list in five out of six semesters, that fact was properly listed. Of course, if the student had made Dean's List only one out of six semesters, the entry would just read: Dean's List. Finally, since everybody knows what a high school valedictorian is, there's no need to explain it. But since this student was ranked first in a class of 650 students, that fact was properly included. If the student was graduated by a high school having thirty members in the senior class, the entry would read: Valedictorian of high school senior class.

Employment

This heading is the one most likely to vary in position, content, and style depending on whether the resume is for an over-thirty working professional, a graduate student, a college student, a homemaker reentering the job market, or a high school student. Keep in mind that you can modify this or any other heading. If you're looking for a computer job and have held computer positions, you can use as a heading Computer Employment or Computer Experience rather than Employment. You can creatively make your own headings, such as Business Experience, Sales Experience, Writing Experience, Legal Employment, School Employment, or Summer Employment. In this discussion, however, we'll refer to the heading as Employment.

What to Include.   For most people the Employment heading should chronologically list employment experiences. Each entry will usually be a particular job with a particular company, but we'll see a bit later certain circumstances that might prompt you to group several jobs in one entry. Each entry should give the name of the employment entity and the city and state where the job was located. You need not include exact addresses of the employers. Each entry should also include the beginning and ending dates of the employment. And most important of all, each entry should describe what you did and what you accomplished.

Position.   Each entry might also reveal your position. Certainly you want to give the position if its name is impressive, like

Executive Vice President or even Research Assistant. But if your position title was Clerk B or Law Firm Runner, then you should exclude it. Finally, if your job didn't really have a position name, it's perfectly okay for you to make up a name as long as it accurately and honestly reflects what you did.

Accomplishments. Those limp resumes out there wearing grungy old blue jeans will just list the employer, the city and state, the dates, and the position. They will make no attempt to cater to the prospective employer's interests, and they won't toot the horn of the applicant. If you want a properly dressed resume, one that gets noticed, one that opens doors, you need to be prepared to look carefully at your jobs. You need to identify what you accomplished and how those accomplishments relate to the attributes employers want.

When you write the Employment entries, keep your audience in mind. When you describe what you did, be sure to describe what you accomplished. What results did you achieve? Did you meet deadlines? Did you set any records? What was the dollar volume of your sales? Did you respond effectively to customers? Did you achieve a turnaround of a previously losing situation? Did you creatively change an old procedure, or initiate a new one? How much money did you handle each day? Each week? Each month? During the entire job? Did you work overtime? Did you hold more than one job simultaneously? For summer jobs, were you asked to return to the same job for future summers because of your demonstrated success? Whatever you did, no matter how menial you think it might sound, you must have accomplished something.

Traps to Avoid. Of all the headings in a resume, the Employment section causes the most trouble and prompts the most questions. There are two types of information you typically exclude from this section: pay and reason for leaving. As a general rule, do not include your pay scale. This is especially true for student summer jobs where the rate of pay is next to irrelevant. Who needs to know you made $4.25 an hour? And at any level, listing salary invites misinterpretation. You may be making $25,000 annually for work that could get you $40,000 elsewhere; although the reason may be that you negotiated your current situation badly or that your organization just won't pay more, the reader of the resume may conclude that your work is at the $25,000 level. So if you're changing jobs, typically you will not include your salary. After all, you're changing jobs to get a higher salary, right? If you reveal your current salary, prospective employers may think they can pick you up for a steal.

When you go in for your interview and are asked to fill out an employment application, you will then probably reveal your current or previous salary. So the point isn't to withhold salary information indefinitely, only long enough so that you get the interview and a situation where you can explain your salary history in person.

Excluding salary is not a hard and fast rule, however. We remember well the resume of a highly successful manufacturer's representative for a textile company in North Carolina. He had begun his sales career earning $12,000. Then he jumped to $18,000. Then to $24,000. Then to $36,000. Then to $60,000. He had increased his salary by 500 percent in just seven years. When we wrote each entry, we prominently displayed the salary for each position. The message was clear: "I'm on the move. If you want me, make me an offer. It'd better be good."

Neither is the rule inflexible for student summer jobs. We once worked with a college senior who wanted to get a sales position. Did he have any experience? You bet. During the previous summer he had sold books door-to-door. Big deal, you say. Well, in three months he sold $24,000 worth of books. His net pay? Over $10,000. Not bad, huh. He prominently revealed his compensation for his summer work. Recruiters fell all over themselves making this guy an offer.

Another trap: reason for leaving. We're surprised so many people put this down on their resumes. Frankly, prior to the interview, it's none of the recruiters' business why you left a particular job. Of course, if they grant you an interview, they can and will ask why you left a particular position, and you should be ready to answer that question.

A few years ago, we worked with a young woman from Ohio who wanted to land a consultant's position with a New York City firm. She had held a consulting position for four years, but the current employer was letting her go. That's right. She was given notice to be out by November. During the preceding summer we helped her with her resume and a highly ambitious direct mail campaign. On the resume we listed quite truthfully the dates of the current position as "1980 to present." Not a word did we say about the impending job termination. We then produced more than 1,000 personally typed letters to firms in the metropolitan New York area. The result? She got more than twenty interviews. Naturally no one thought to ask, "Are you about to be fired?" The reason for leaving never came up. She's now happily working in New York earning $12,000 more than she earned at the previous company.

That's the way it should be done. Never, ever put negative information on your resume. If you were fired from a job and the question comes up in an interview, then you answer directly and honestly. But you are under absolutely no obligation to reveal bad information unless you're asked. And since nobody's asking anything when you write your resume, you have no ethical obligation to blow your horn with a sour note.

Let us anticipate some further questions.

Describing the Typical College Student Summer Job.   You had summer jobs slinging hash, mowing yards, and babysitting. Most college students sling hash, mow yards, and sit babies. Right off the bat you can feel a little more comfortable that the odds are with you. The college recruiters will be seeing an overwhelming number of resumes that say: "Waited tables and helped in the kitchen." You can make yours different by thinking about your accomplishments slinging hash. You figure out what you did well on that summer job. Keeping the sixteen attributes in mind, you then describe how you "worked effectively waiting tables, providing personal service to customers, dealing positively with complaints, and calmly operating in a pressure-cooker environment."

Suppose, however, you didn't really provide much personal service to customers. Suppose the job was not a pressure cooker. It was boring. Why did you take the job? You needed the money. So don't describe the job much at all. Just say you "worked full-time waiting tables to earn enough funds to return to college." This shows you had a goal of getting a college education and were willing to do the drudge work necesssary to pay for it (goal achievement).

What if you held the same job for more than one summer? Then you've got a real opportunity to score some points on your resume. After all, here's an employer who has recognized your ability and has asked you to return. Were you given a raise when you returned? Were you given more responsibility? If so, be sure to say so. Your entry might look like this:

| Employment: | <u>The Foot Locker,</u> Butte, Montana. Summers 1989, 1990, 1991. Initially employed in high school to work as a sales clerk. Due to successful performance I was asked to return for two additional summers at a higher rate of pay with added responsibility. Ranked as the #2 salesperson during the first summer and advanced to #1 the next two summers. Assisted in arranging eye-catching retail displays; served as manager of other summer workers during owner's absence. |

Many Positions for the Same Employer. This same technique should be used by professionals and other workers who are seeking a job change. If you've been with an organization for quite some time, you should view that as a strength. It shows loyalty and staying power. Your Employment entry should lead with the name of the company and then show your consistent advancement to higher positions. Thus, your entry might look like this:

| Employment: | **Acme International Widgets, Inc.,** Pittsburgh, PA. In five years I received three promotions all with added pay and increased responsibility. 1980–present. |

Production Line Manager. Promoted to manage all facets of production including direct supervision of 25 foremen and 150 workers. Instituted new cost control systems resulting in a total annual saving of $225,000. 1983–present.

Quality Control Supervisor. Promoted to supervise all quality control systems employed in the manufacture of more than $2,500,000 of widgets annually. Supervised 15 quality control inspectors. Created and instituted a new random check system that reduced shipment of defective widgets by 25%. 1981–1983.

Quality Control Inspector. Served as one of 15 inspectors for one year before promotion to a position supervising all inspectors. 1980–1981.

Dealing with a Whole Bunch of Jobs. Many people have held a host of jobs. Even college students might have held numerous positions during the school years, school vacations, and summers. If you devote an entire entry to each job, three bad things can happen. First, your resume looks cluttered. Second, your resume is too long. And third, your resume gives the impression you've jumped around from job to job. The first two problems involve content and appearance. The third, if true, presents more serious concerns for the prospective employer.

One way around these problems is to lump several jobs in one resume entry, which typically should be the last entry under the Employment heading. We can best demonstrate the procedure by giving an example. We were working with a real estate manager who needed a resume to apply for a once-in-a-lifetime job opportunity. Within the previous eighteen months he had been affiliated with three different real estate brokerage firms. He had listed each one on his resume, giving the visual and substantive impression that he was a job hopper. It turned out that he hadn't really hopped from job to job. Rather, he had moved to the area recently, possessed a valid real estate license from the state, and had affiliated with three different firms until a permanent position materialized. But his resume gave the appearance of an unstable individual, despite his otherwise impressive real estate career.

To repair the damage we lumped his last three positions into one graphically plain entry as follows:

Recent Real Estate Experience: After moving to the Shenandoah Valley I affiliated with three real estate firms for the past 18 months to specialize in the sale of farm properties. Even as a newcomer to the area, generated sales exceeding $1,000,000 during this period.

Anyone having a whole bunch of jobs can use the same technique to reduce the number of entries required to show employment history. After chronologically detailing the more important positions you've held, you could include one entry as follows:

Other Positions: Since sophomore year in high school, have worked full-time during each summer and all school vacations and part-time during the academic years. Positions included short-order cook, landscape maintenance helper at a large apartment complex, delivery driver for a pizza business, and night watchman at a manufacturing facility.

This technique also works for jobs that precede your work in your current field, or jobs that seem too far back and unrelated to your field to be of much significance. For example, a clinical psychologist started out working in secretarial positions before she went back to school to get her graduate degree. After chronologically detailing the positions she has held in her profession, she might include one entry as follows:

Other Positions: Before earning my Masters in Clinical Psychology, worked as a secretary in a brokerage firm, administrative assistant for a magazine publisher, and editorial secretary for a book publisher, in Los Angeles, 1966–75.

Over Thirty: The Functional Subheading Resume. People who have worked for one employer for many years typically have trouble describing their many positions, many locations, and many duties and responsibilities. For the past several years, we've been invited to participate in the United States Secret Service Retirement seminars. Typically, these Secret Service agents have spent twenty years with the government and are now ready to retire. Most, of course, are ready to strike out in new directions in second careers. Their long tenure with one employer causes all sorts of resume-writing problems, which we've found are effectively solved by the functional subheading resume introduced in Chapter 3.

When reviewing the resumes of some of these seminar participants, we have noticed that they tend to view each position held with the Secret Service as a separate job. Thus, their entire Secret Service careers are stretched out over several posts or assignments or positions. In these various positions, the typical agent would perform the same kinds of duties and responsibilities. The resume writers, therefore, find themselves saying the same things over and over again for each position in each post where they served.

Military personnel often face the same dilemma. Careers stretching over twenty years tend to yield a host of positions in a wide variety of cities. These careers tend to yield an overly long resume detailing each position, each location, and each set of (mostly similar) duties and responsibilities. The solution to this resume-writing dilemma, the functional subheading resume, is one of the best ways to organize a varied career. Suppose you've served in six different locations in six different positions, but that your duties all involved one activity: recruiting. A typical chronological resume would work backward in time, listing each of the six positions in each of the six locations and describing what duties were involved in each assignment. Naturally, the duties were similar if not identical, so the resume writer says essentially the same thing in six consecutive entries, boring the resume reviewer to tears!

The better way to present this experience is to look carefully at the market you're trying to crack and ask yourself this question: "What three or four traits or abilities does my future employer want me to have?" Our resume writer, the recruiter, might answer:

1. Recruiting and interviewing experience
2. Managerial ability
3. Marketing and promotions

Knowing this, the resume writer adapts these abilities as functional subheadings to portray vividly and graphically exactly what the employer is looking for. Of course, in describing each functional subheading the resume writer might be drawing from the experience gained at any or all of the six assignments. Here's what the functional subheading approach might look like:

Personnel Experience: **UNITED STATES ARMY RECRUITER,** 1967–present. Served for 16 years in various capacities to support and implement the U.S. Army's recruitment effort to satisfy personnel needs of an all-volunteer Army. Positions ranged from Personnel Recruiter to Chief Recruiter in charge of an office of six recruiters, two staff members, and various part-time employees. Gained significant experience in the following areas:

- *Recruiting & Interviewing Experience.* Visited scores of local high schools and colleges to present career opportunities to young men and women. Conducted in-depth interviews with prospective recruits, ascertaining their abilities and areas of technical or academic expertise to fill a wide variety of positions.
- *Managerial Ability.* Supervised the entire operation at the U.S. Army Recruitment Office in Kansas City, Missouri. Took charge of overall administrative duties, built an effective team of recruiters and administrative staff, and consistently met or exceeded recruitment goals.

- *Marketing & Promotions.* Created a telemarketing program to contact high school seniors
to inquire about their post-graduate plans.
Followed up each call with a direct mail campaign to provide printed literature on Army opportunities. The program netted a 25% increase
in prospective recruits in just six months.

You can easily see how this functional subheading approach enables you to organize your experience, to present just the information about your accomplishments and abilities that targets your market, and to impress your prospective employer that you've got exactly what it takes to get the job done.

Homemakers Reentering the Job Market. For returning home-makers, the sound of the word employment may be enough to make your toes curl. "Employment," you say, "I don't have any employment. That's my problem. I need employment, but I've never done anything. For pay, that is."

Without doubt, the Employment heading causes the most difficulty for homemakers entering the job market for the first time or after an extended time working twenty-four hours a day as mother, father, or head of household. To make things simple, we'll focus this discussion on those entering the job market with little or no employment history. Of course, you've probably held some jobs at some point in your life, but you've concluded that they're too ancient or unrelated to be of much value on your resume.

Perhaps you went to high school, graduated, had some college, or perhaps even some graduate school. That's good. You got married, maybe even had children. That's even better. But truth be known, you've collected few paychecks in your life. That's the problem with your life right now. You've baked enough bread to feed Poland. Time now to win some of it back.

So what do you put in your Employment heading? "All those silly jobs I held light years ago when I was in high school and wore a size six with room to spare?" Nope. Nothing. You omit the Employment heading altogether.

"A resume without the Employment heading?" you ask. "But that will show I haven't had any work experience."

The employer is going to find that out anyway. You could include the Employment heading and stuff it up with those jobs you had back in high school. Go ahead and wow the employers with your ability to operate a popcorn machine at the Grand Theatre or your knack for tearing tickets into two precisely equal halves. But will that do you any good? Not likely.

Instead, why not create alternative headings that show employers that you've got some valuable skills, abilities, or even traits for sale? Scour your background for evidence of the sixteen attributes employers are looking for. Hammer home the organizational ability you showed in the youth soccer league you headed. Zero in on the leadership you showed serving groups as president, vice-president, secretary, or treasurer. Tout the communication skills you demonstrated in the oral presentations you made before the local school board. Look thoroughly at your past. Somewhere you'll find value, worth, abilities, and traits employers are willing to pay for.

The list of alternative headings is a mile long. You might consider these or make up your own:

Leadership Ability	Managerial Ability
Writing Skills	Volunteer Work
Organizational Ability	Interpersonal Skills
Attention to Detail	Political Work

High School Students: Babysitting, Lawn Mowing, and Other Excitement.   High school students have a special problem when preparing their resumes to get their first "real" job. Sure, you've done some odd jobs, mowed a few yards, sat a few babies, ran a few errands. But as a rule you haven't had a "real" job. You don't have any eye-catching leads. You haven't worked for any impressive-looking employers. Perhaps your only employer is Mrs. Johnson, the next-door neighbor who, though nice, surely wouldn't look good on your resume. So what should you do? Downplay the Employment heading. Put it last on your resume, and use other headings to strut your stuff. If you've been active in band, soccer, and scouting, then use a lot of resume space by inventing a heading for each of them: Band Activities, Athletics, and Scouting Activities. By eating up some space with these activities and accomplishments, you will have impressed the employer before it dawns on her that your employment record is virtually nonexistent.

Here's what part of your resume might look like:

Band Activities:	**Glendale High School Marching Band,** Glendale, Ohio. Played trombone in award-winning marching band that competed in numerous competitions in Ohio and throughout the midwest.
	Consistently received the grade of *A*. Regularly attended after-school practices for two hours per day, four days per week.
Athletics:	**Glendale Varsity Soccer Team** After playing fullback on J.V. team during the 9th and 10th grades, successfully earned a position as the reserve fullback on the varsity team.
Scouting Activities:	**Glendale Boy Scout Troop #404** Actively participated in scouting since age six. Earned numerous merit badges and travelled with my troop for various activities and camping trips.
Employment:	**Lawnmowing:** To earn extra spending money, worked 20 hours per week during the summers mowing lawns for neighbors. Maintained accurate records for tax purposes. Summers 1990–91.
	Babysitting: As early as age 13, served as a babysitter for neighbors; responsible for caring for infants and small children during afternoons and nights. Summers 1988–89.

You can readily see how the above approach helps to fill up your resume and to reveal your typical high school summer jobs.

Employment: A Summary.   Before moving on to Activities, let's summarize the Employment heading. You're using a resume to get employment. One therefore could argue that the Employment heading is the most important of all. For those who have been out of school for more than a year, it is the most important section. Employers want to see whom you've worked for, in what capacity, what you did, and when you did it. For those still in school, the Employment section is important if you've had some appealing employment experience. If you haven't, then you can downplay it as long as you have strength under other headings.

As you write your Employment entries, keep at the forefront of your mind your audience, your prospective employer. You're giving or mailing your resume to someone you want to work for. That employer wants to see not only the positions you've held but also your accomplishments. That employer wants to see evidence of hard work, initiative, responsibility, relevant vocational skills, interpersonal skills, competitiveness, leadership, imagination, goal achievement, stress management, direction, self-knowledge, intelligence, self-confidence, communication skills, and flexibility. If you think about it, all sixteen attributes relate to Employment, although they don't necessarily relate to other headings.

Your task in writing your thirty-second spot is to create an ad in which your strongest attributes leap off the page. You want an eye-catching document that grabs the employment manager's attention. You want a resume that shouts, "Put me in the let's-take-a-look pile! You'll never regret it!"

Show the employer you've got what it takes. Show not just what you did, but what you accomplished. Give that consumer exactly what she wants. The results are guaranteed: you'll get what you want—interviews and ultimately a job.

Activities

If you have been active in the community, public schools, scouting, charities, student groups, a fraternity or sorority, student government, university committees, or student publications, then naturally you should include an Activities heading. If you have not been particularly active in community or extracurricular activities because you've been working, studying, or playing hard, then exclude this heading. If you have some activities, but they are not impressive enough to warrant a separate Activities heading, include them as a subheading under Education.

The Don't-List Rule. When you write the entries for the Activities heading, follow the same procedures I described for the Employment heading. In other words, don't just list the groups you've been affiliated with and the positions you held with those groups. Instead, describe what you accomplished or the purpose of the group (if not evident from the group's name). Thus, don't just list the name of your professional association and your office like this:

Activities: **President,** Santa Barbara Chapter, California Writers Club, 1990–91.

Instead, describe your duties and accomplishments like this:

Activities: **President,** Santa Barbara Chapter, California Writers Club. Planned and directed all meetings of this 120-member professional organization. Arranged speakers and panel participants for meetings, including several bestselling and national prize-winning authors. Launched campaign to increase membership of nationally published authors by 45%. 1990–91.

Similarly, don't list your sorority and your office like this:

Activities: **Phi Phi Phi Sorority,** Rush Chairperson, 1990–91.

Instead, describe your duties and accomplishments like this:

Activities: **Phi Phi Phi Sorority Rush Chairperson.** Coordinated all activities necessary to receive and interview more than 1,500 college women. Presided over sorority meetings to review candidates' credentials and select a pledge class of 25 members. 1991–92.

If you've been extraordinarily active, you should resist the urge to include every organization you've been associated with.

A resume that lists every activity you've had will be too cluttered and boring. Instead, select the most impressive and devote your resume space to showing your specific accomplishments.

College students, remember that you may include high school activities if they are particularly impressive. If you've chosen to include your high school under the Education heading, you might reveal your activities in that entry. Otherwise, you may divide the Activities heading into two subheadings, one named College and the other High School. Then describe your activities accordingly.

High school students, as previously shown, will use your Activities as the primary material for your resume. You want to stretch out the activities you do have to fill up your resume.

Everybody else, if space is at a premium in your resume, you might decide to violate the don't-list rule. Certainly in some situations you can simply list the names of your activities, especially when prospective employers know full well what the activities entail. For example, a law student might just list his moot court participation and how far he advanced in the competition. Attorneys know what moot court is all about. Other disciplines undoubtedly have similar groups so well known within the profession that a simple listing of the activity sends the right message to the employer.

Modifying Activities.   Finally, keep in mind that you can effectively modify the Activities heading, especially when you are targeting your resume to a particular profession. Thus, the person seeking a job in publishing can modify the heading to Writing Activities. Don't shy away from being creative and including such headings as Political Activities, Marketing Activities, or Drama Activities.

Additional Headings

Athletics.   Remember competition? Employers like that trait. It definitely shows up in the sports world. If you've competed in varsity athletics in high school or college, you probably should include an Athletics heading. Or if you are genuinely active in athletic activities not connected with high school or college, you probably should include the Athletics heading as well. For example, if you've competed in some marathons but were not on the college track team, you might decide to include an Athletics heading. If your only athletic activity is participation in college intramural sports, you probably should not include a separate Athletics heading. Instead, if you're still a student or are a graduating student, include your intramural experiences, if at all, under the Activities heading.

Community Service.   This heading might also be called Volunteer Work. It should be included in your resume if you've done any significant work in the community that shows you are the joiner type or the public service type.

Companies are acutely aware of their community images. Indeed, they employ full-time people to look after their community affairs. They know their business image will benefit if their managers and other employees are active in the community. If you have a public service streak in you, you should display your accomplishments in this heading.

Be careful in deciding which activities to include and in writing the entries. Community service is likely to involve politics or religion, which can be sensitive areas in your own life and in the lives of your prospective employers. For example, if you're trying to crack into one of the Big Eight accounting firms, we'd counsel against including an entry like, "volunteer work with the Weathermen underground, organizing demonstrations against capitalistic exploitation." (One law student at the University of Virginia touted her left-wing political groups while simultaneously trying to crack into conservative Wall Street law firms. She did not succeed.)

Travel.   If you've never been beyond the next county, forget this heading. If, however, you're a student and you spent an entire summer camping out in the far West or have visited foreign countries, then you should include a Travel or Foreign Travel heading. A single entry should suffice, describing your travel experiences and listing the countries or states you've visited.

For any others, if you're interested in careers in international relations or international business, a prominently displayed Foreign Travel heading can alert your prospective employer to your ability to adjust to foreign cultures. Be sure to include the amount of time you've spent abroad (if that amount is impressive). Also, if you've made several trips abroad, include the circumstances and the number of trips.

One of the participants in the Secret Service retirement seminars was seeking a position in international security. As a Secret Service agent, he had traveled extensively in foreign countries, hobnobbed with upper-level government officials, was fluent in two languages, and had worked with foreign police agencies conducting innumerable investigations. Naturally, we wrote a prominent entry describing his international experience to show his ability to function at many levels in many cultures.

Military Service.   If you've served in the military, include this heading. Be sure to include the branch of the service, the places where you were stationed, your rank, any medals received, and any special training or skills you acquired. As with other headings, your entry should show accomplishments that reflect the sixteen attributes employers seek.

When writing the Military Service entry, try to get rid of military jargon, and write like a normal person. Your audience will appreciate it.

Military personnel should study our other book, *Does Your Resume Wear Combat Boots?* also published by Prima Publishing.

Languages.   If you're seeking a job that values foreign language ability and you have impressive ability in one or more languages, then definitely include this heading. The entry should list the languages and reveal your degree of proficiency. Be very careful with the word fluent, however. Nothing could be worse than to say you're fluent in French, get an interview, and look dumbfounded as the interviewer begins by saying: *"Bonjour, Mademoiselle. C'est magnifique de parler avec vous aujourd'hui."*

If you have extraordinary ability in languages and seek an international position, don't be afraid to toot your horn. We once worked with one student who was fluent in French, German, Italian, and Polish. He prominently included the Foreign Language heading, which said: "Fluent in French, German, Italian, and Polish (see attached)." Then, on an attached sheet, he thoroughly described his foreign language experience by revealing the extent of his formal schooling and his experience in the foreign countries themselves.

Keep in mind that fluency in a foreign language can be an asset even if you're not applying for a foreign post. Certainly a fluency in Spanish would open the eyes of a prospective employer in Miami or any other area of the country with a large Hispanic population.

Do not include computer programming languages such as COBOL, FORTRAN, BASIC, and Pascal under the Languages heading. At least modify the heading to Computer Languages. Also, in listing your computer languages, be sure to use all caps for those that are acronyms, like BASIC, COBOL, FORTRAN, and upper- and lowercase for those that are not, like Pascal.

Publications.   If you've written an article, poem, or anything else that has been published, you should include this heading. Remember that employers seek communication skills! In the entry, list the titles of the publications and follow your discipline's citation form.

Interests.   Opinion differs on the effectiveness of this heading. Some experts say to leave it out altogether. Others say definitely to include it. Our advice falls somewhere in between.

You should be creative when you write the Interests heading, if you have some genuinely interesting interests. If you just list "Jogging, Music, and Reading," the employer will yawn. Everybody these days jogs, listens to music (while jogging), and reads (jogging books). If that's all you're really interested in, then leave the heading out. Or, make your routine interests sound interesting with an entry like, "Jogging five miles per day, reading spy novels, and listening to classical and country music."

Several years ago I worked with an extremely talented young woman who was writing her first resume. She had omitted the Interests heading. I asked whether she had any unique outside interests. She replied, "Hot-air ballooning." Naturally, I revised her resume to include this short statement:

Interests: Hot-air ballooning.

I recently heard from my hot-air balloonist friend, who's now the head paralegal at a large insurance company, and she reports that her Interests heading has always sparked some lively conversation in interviews.

Personal.   The Personal heading is where most job seekers shoot themselves right in the foot. Remember, recruiters will use resumes as disqualifiers to reduce the number of viable candidates for a position. The way not to disqualify yourself on paper is to avoid providing extraneous information that doesn't add to your qualifications in any way.

Most personal information is considered privileged anyway and cannot be used to make a hiring decision under the Equal Employment Opportunity laws. Race, creed, ethnic origin (citizenship or legal entry are required questions), and gender may not be used to make a hiring decision. There are some exceptions to this rule, generally in some federal agencies, but most companies do not even ask the questions.

If a company asks you your age and then fails to hire you, you might assume the only reason you were not selected was because you were too old or too young. The interesting point is that if you provided a resume including any personal information, you would never know why the company did not call you. Even if the recruiter did use some discriminatory screening process, you would never know it. The solution is not to include personal information that is not needed to determine your qualifications.

Some examples of items to keep off your resume:

Photos.   One recent innovation in resume preparation is the reproduction of a photograph on the resume itself. The problem is that your idea of what is attractive may not be the same as the recruiter's. In fact, you might be ugly as sin and not even know it! Pictures don't add to your qualifications (unless you are an actor or a model). But see our exception to the no-photo rule in Chapter 3.

Clubs. You may be proud that you are an active member of a fraternal or civic organization. But certain fraternal and civic organizations discriminate in membership requirements, as some recent court cases have attested. The person reading your resume could have been refused membership in the organization, or may belong to another organization with opposing views. Including your club might prompt the resume screener to omit your resume from the let's-take-a-look pile.

Height and Weight. You might be very proud of the fact that you are 5'2", eyes of blue, and weigh 175 pounds. But the recruiter reading your resume might hate to look at short, fat guys. You wouldn't get called.

Smoking. The latest hot issue in the employment industry is the smoking problem. 73 percent of companies recently surveyed by a national publication indicated that if an applicant smoked during the interview it would reflect unfavorably on the hiring decision. Does that mean you should indicate on your resume that you are a nonsmoker? How can you be sure the recruiter doesn't smoke? One corporate recruiter uses only one match a day—to light his first of an unbroken chain of cigarettes. This person is sick of hearing others nag him to quit, and he is not interested in bringing more nonsmokers onto the staff. Smokers go to the top of his let's-take-a-look pile.

Marital Status. Marital status obviously has nothing to do with your ability to perform a job, but some people don't see it that way. For example, a married person is considered to be stable, a divorced person unstable. A single person might be stable or unstable (they might get married and move). Along the same lines, children do not add to or detract from your abilities, so an entry that states that you have "three wonderful children, aged 10, 12, and 14" generally will not get your resume to the top of the pile. Further, single parents are sometimes perceived to be a potential problem because they might have to run off to care for their children. In reality, many people know single parents are generally better time managers than people in two-parent families. They have to be. But they might not get an opportunity to prove it unless they get called for the interview.

Social Security Number.   Leave it out.

So what should be included? Here are some suggestions:

Name, Address, and Telephone Number.   We have a resume in our files from a former Marine that only lists his name, with no address or phone number. He had paid $175 to have that resume prepared. When we pointed out the omission, the Marine said, "No wonder I haven't heard from anyone."

Your name should appear on every page, in case the pages get separated. The address should be one where you can be reached. The telephone number should be one that will be answered during normal business hours. If there is no one to answer the phone, invest in an answering machine and make sure you leave a professional-sounding message on the machine. Be careful about a child who likes to play with the phone and who may cause you to miss a message. College and graduate students, be very careful during job-search season with your highly creative, musical, and perhaps obscene answering-machine messages. You don't want to be singing Be-Bop-A-Lula to a prospective corporate employer.

Security Clearance.   List the highest clearance you have ever held, any special access you may have had (that you can reveal), and the date of your last update.

Place of Birth.   Again, apply the does-it-help? test. If you want a job in Philadelphia and were born and raised in the area, then say under the Personal heading, "Born and raised in the Philadelphia area."

Availability Date.   The job search will usually begin before you are available for a new position, so you should tell the employer when you can start work. Do not write, "Immediately." That implies that you are unemployed, and, for some strange reason, employers feel people who already have jobs are more valuable. If you are unemployed, indicate that you are available "with reasonable notice."

Health.   Even if you aren't quite up to snuff, you should write, "Health: Excellent." If the disability does not impede your ability to perform the task, then your health is excellent. We recommend that you always include this statement, especially if you are over forty. Recruiters play the same kind of reverse-thinking games we are discussing here. If you omit the statement, they might assume something is wrong with you. We should note, of course, that the new Americans With Disabilities Act outlaws any employment decisions based on disabilities.

Age.   There is obvious age discrimination in the private-sector workforce. The problem is that you really won't know if the company you are applying to prefers younger workers. This entry is not required on a resume and should not be used to make a hiring decision. However, it could work for or against you. The best advice is to omit age unless it is used to clarify other information. For example, if you are a very young person and have accomplished a tremendous amount in a few short years, you might want to list your age to show your youth. If you are very young and feel the position requires someone with more maturity, leave it out. Conversely, if you are older and the position apparently is designed for youth, or if you are older and have few qualifications, omit age.

Other Personal Information.   You should leave off most other personal information. If personal information about you passes the does-it-help? test, then you may include a heading entitled Personal or Personal Background to reveal any personal items that favor you or that are related to your qualifications.

References

Most resumes will end with the References heading. And they end in a whimper. They fizzle out and say, "References: Available on request." Or they use a fancier preposition and say, "Available upon request." Or they say, "Furnished upon request." Of course references are available on request. What are you going to do when a prospective employer asks for references? Say no? At least you should be a little more upbeat than "Available on request." Instead write, "Excellent references furnished on request." Or you can write, "Professional and personal references provided on request." At least try to end with a bang, not a whimper.

Should you list references on your resume? Experts disagree, but we think you should list your references, either on your resume or on a separate sheet, if those references are recognizable by name or by title. We were working with a student once. We had completed his resume, and we asked if he wanted to list references. "What kind?" he asked. "Well," we said, "do you have anybody who would recommend you and who is recognizable by name or title?" He then proceeded to name a United States senator and a United States congressman, whom he had known all his life. Naturally, those names, addresses, and telephone numbers went down on his resume.

If someone famous will recommend you, put the name on your resume. Is it name dropping to do so? You bet it is, and it works. Alternatively, if someone with a spiffy title will recommend you, put the name, title, address, and phone number on your resume. Spiffy titles include: Professor, Dean, President, Owner, Manager, and so on.

If you decide to list references, be sure you personally call them and ask their permission. Make certain you tell each reference you intend to include his or her name, address, and phone number on your resume. When your resume is complete, be sure to send a copy to each reference along with a short thank-you note.

One effective alternative to listing your references directly on your resume is to have a separate reference sheet. In this way you can send out resumes that do not reveal names and addresses of your references and then present the reference sheet at the interview. Or you might decide some prospective employers should receive references at the same time they receive your resume. Then you include the reference sheet with that mailing.

Sequencing Information

We've just reviewed the various headings that might appear in a chronological resume. Before you begin to put your resume together, however, you must make some decisions about the sequence of your headings. What comes first? What last? Two rules should govern your sequencing decision: First, lead with your strength. Second, end with a bang. To understand each of these rules, remember that employers read resumes in thirty seconds. If an employer is going to scan your resume, you don't want to bury your strongest point in the body or at the bottom. Let's take a careful look at how you might sequence your headings. Then we'll study effective techniques of writing attention-grabbing leads.

Remember that all resumes must have a caption, and that it comes first. So your name, address or addresses, and telephone number or numbers should appear at the top of your resume. If you've decided to include an objective or its substitute, the personal profile, then by tradition it should come first. Following that, your first heading should be your most impressive credential. If you're currently enrolled in or were recently graduated by a well-known and respected college or university, the Education heading most likely will be the first. But suppose your college is impressive, but you have another terrifically impressive credential. In that case you might position the other credential as the first heading.

Let's turn the situation around. Suppose your college just isn't all that impressive. Suppose you have some impressive work experience and some solid honors and awards. Do you put Education at the top? Definitely not. You might even decide to put Education near the bottom.

To sequence your headings properly you must critically examine your life and objectively determine your relative strengths. The strongest aspect of your life should be the first heading. Make the next heading the second most impressive thing about you. And so on down into the resume.

Inventing Headings or Subheadings

We once helped a student attending the University of Virginia put together his resume. Ordinarily he would put the Education heading first. But this student, who was seeking a position in sales, had sold $24,000 worth of books door-to-door the previous summer. His other employment experience, however, was a series of typical college student summer jobs. He didn't want to include Employment as the first heading because it would shove his University of Virginia credential to the middle of the resume. Quite correctly he wanted it near the top. But he also wanted the sales job at the top. So he devised his own heading called Sales Experience, and listed it first. Since it took up very little room, his next heading, Education, kept the University of Virginia credential near the top of the resume. Then, further down in the resume, he included an Employment heading, which took care of his typical summer jobs.

You too should carefully look at your experiences, especially at your jobs. You might have some ho-hum jobs and some spiffy jobs. The trouble is, the spiffy job is not the most recent, and in a chronological format you can't lead with your strength. Be creative, and reposition information in your resume so that your strong credentials appear near the top.

Let's look at another example. Suppose your most recent job was last summer slinging hash at the university diner. The previous spring, however, you served as a research assistant for a professor. In a chronological resume the hash job appears first, the research job second. But why not divide the Employment heading into two subheadings, one called School Employment, the other Summer Employment? Then list School Employment first. That way the research job gets top billing, and you shove the hash-slinging job down in the resume.

Ending with a Bang

Of course the only problem with ordering your headings by their relative impressiveness is that you end your resume with a whimper and not a bang. Why do you want to end with a bang? Well, think about the way people scan written material such as an article. They look quickly at the stuff at the top, then skim over the stuff in the middle, and finally take a peek at the end. If recruiters will take a peek at the end of your resume, it makes sense to end your resume with a bang.

By tradition, References is the last heading in the resume. If you decide to include the heading but exclude the names, one way to end with a bang is to create something other than, "Available upon request." At least you can say, "Excellent references are available on request." One student's resume said this under References: "Gladly furnished."

If you decide to include the names and addresses of your references, presumably those names will constitute the necessary bang. Be sure your references are recognizable by name or title, of course.

Finally, there are two additional tricks you can use to end with a bang. First, reserve an important heading for positioning at the bottom. Likely candidates might be Travel, Languages, or Athletics. Second, you can use the footnote technique: somewhere in your resume when you're tempted to put in a really strong fact about yourself, resist that temptation and put the fact in a footnote. Suppose you have a 3.2 GPA. Under the Education heading you're writing your college entry. You're tempted to write: "Overall GPA of 3.2 earned while working 20 hours per week during the academic year." Now that's a good bit of information in that entry. But what you might do instead is this: "Overall GPA = 3.2*" Then at the bottom of your resume you write this:

*Earned 3.2 GPA while working 20 hours per week during the academic year.

"Hmmm, hard worker, smart, clever," muses the employment manager as she puts your resume in the let's-take-a-look pile

pile. We've seen the same technique used to reveal simultaneous jobs held, sales record achieved, prizes won, and a host of other extremely strong information. It's a good technique, and definitely gets attention.

Creating Leads

Let me refresh your memory of the terms headings, entries, and leads. The heading is the word or words categorizing your life, such as Education, Activities, Employment, and so on. Entries are blocks of information within a heading, such as schools attended, jobs held, activities undertaken, and so on. Leads are the first words of each entry. And leads are extraordinarily important: they draw the eye of the resume reviewer to an entry, capture the employer's attention, and pique his curiosity. Yet most people blow their leads.

Don't Blow Your Leads

Remember this rule: lead with your strength. That rule applies to sequencing headings, but it also applies to your leads. The lead for each entry should be the strongest point about yourself. So that you understand this vital function of leads, let's look at some examples.

Suppose you attend a well-respected college. The lead for that entry most likely will be the name of the college. Thus, your lead under the Education heading would look like this:

Education: **HARVARD COLLEGE,** Cambridge, Massachusetts. B.A. in History, May 1985. Curriculum required extensive independent research and writing. GPA in major = 3.1.

In that entry the emphasized lead makes the credential leap off the page. Remember, the employer is devoting about thirty seconds in the first resume review. All you want to do at first is to get in the let's-take-a-look pile.

Suppose, on the other hand, that our Harvard student wants a job in the computer industry and is about to receive a B.S. in Computer Science. The student might decide to lead with the degree instead of the name of the school. So the heading, entry, and lead would look like this:

Education: **B.S. IN COMPUTER SCIENCE,** Harvard College, Cambridge, MA. Degree expected May 1993. Computer courses included Assembly Language, BASIC, FORTRAN, and Pascal. Senior computer project entailed developing and testing an inventory control system for a small business.

In the Education heading your lead should be either the name of the school or the name of the degree, depending on which one is the more impressive or more directly relevant to the job you seek.

People also tend to blow their leads in the Employment heading. The problem usually crops up either with position titles or dates. Look at the following two examples:

Employment: **CLERK B, Department of Agriculture,** Washington, DC. Worked during the summer as a typist. General office duties. Summer 1991.

Employment: **6/8/91–8/27/91,** Clerk B, Department of Agriculture, Washington, DC. Worked in the summer as a typist. General office duties.

In these examples the resume writers blew their leads. Is the employer impressed that the first person was a Clerk B? Does the employer even care that the second person began work on the eighth of June and ended on the twenty-seventh of August? No, to both questions. In each example the writer broke the rule of leading with strength. The strength, of course, is the Department of Agriculture. The heading, lead, and entry should look like this:

Employment: **U.S. DEPARTMENT OF AGRICULTURE,**
Washington, DC. Worked in the office of Director
of Farm Programs. Provided effective clerical
assistance; observed the operations of a major
government department; interacted with top
officials. Summer 1991.

Notice that the resume writer didn't even mention the position, Clerk B. Why? Because Clerk B just isn't very exciting. The strength lay not in the position but in the name of the employment entity. The lead, then, is the entity, not the position.

Honestly Inventing a Position as a Lead

Let's turn the problem around. Suppose you worked for Buffalo Bob's. Doesn't exactly send shivers up your spine, does it? Suppose your job was to assist the manager and owner of this highly popular men's clothing store specializing in western attire. You really didn't have a position. You just helped the owner and did what you were told to do. What's your lead? Buffalo Bob's? No! Your lead looks like this:

Employment: **ASSISTANT TO THE MANAGER,** Buffalo Bob's,
Fairfax, Virginia. Worked 40 hours per week as
the right-hand assistant of the owner and manager
of a popular men's clothing store specializing in
western attire. Gained significant experience in
retailing, including direct contact with clientele,
retail displays, inventory, and promotions.
Summer 1991.

Or suppose you had a position that was given a strange technical title by the organization when the real position's normal title would be more impressive or more understandable. For example, you were called Information Officer B at a large university's business school, but your job was to edit all of the faculty's publications. You were in fact the faculty's editor. Then you're justified in portraying your lead as follows:

Employment: **EDITOR,** Colgate Darden Graduate School of
Business Administration, University of Virginia,
Charlottesville, VA. Edited and proofed textbooks,
articles, research reports, and cases studies submitted by faculty. 1986–88.

Switching Leads

Some situations demand that you switch your leads. For some
jobs you might lead with the employer because the name of
the employer is more impressive. For other jobs, however, the
name of your position is far more impressive than the name
of the employer. Can you switch leads? Why not? You're writing the resume. You're creating your thirty-second message.
You're in control, displaying your life in the strongest possible
way. Will the employer hold your lead switching against you?
No, in the thirty-second scan that initially determines your
fate, the employer will receive the messages you want the employer to receive. The employer won't even notice the apparent
inconsistency.

   To summarize the Employment heading, you should lead
with the employment entity or the position, whichever is more
impressive. Rarely should you lead with the date. You should
use the same strategy to develop any leads for any other entries
in any other headings. In the Activities heading you lead with
the name of the group as a rule. But if you held an impressive
office, then lead with the position. In all events, lead with your
strength!

Problems with Dates

For some reason people get fixated on dates when they write
their resumes. Generally, they put them in the strangest places
and include them for practically every breath they've taken in
their lives. As a general rule you need only document the year
you were graduated or will be graduated by a particular school

and the beginning and ending dates of your employment positions. You do not have to put a date for each office you held in each organization in college. Such information is virtually meaningless. Employers want and need to know when you received or will receive a college degree. They want and need to know how long you lasted at each job. They do not need or want to know when you served as rush chairperson for Phe Phi Pho Phum Fraternity.

Where to Put Dates

Before you can decide where to put education and employment dates, you first have to decide whether that information is important enough to emphasize or, frankly, to hide. For example, if you've worked every summer since your sophomore year in high school, you might want to emphasize dates to show that you're accustomed to hard work. On the other hand, if you have some embarrassing gaps in your employment, you certainly don't want to emphasize your embarrassment by highlighting dates. By the same token, if you've been out of college for a few years and stayed with one awful job for only a short time, you don't want to emphasize the beginning and ending dates of that job or you'll look like a job hopper.

First decide on the relative strength of your dates. If the dates are positive, then highlight them. If the dates are negative, then hide them. If the dates are irrelevant, then include them but don't draw attention to them. You can highlight strong dates by placing them in the left-hand margin or even by using the dates as leads. Take a look at the next two examples where the resume writer wants to emphasize dates.

Employment: **Artistic Director,** Norfolk Theater Festival.
1974–87   Planned, organized, and managed the most
                          popular theater series in the Tidewater Virginia
                          metropolitan region, producing at least seven plays
                          and musicals a season for 14 consecutive
                          summers.

Employment: <u>**1974–87. Artistic Director,**</u> Norfolk Theater
Festival. Planned, organized, and managed the
most popular theater series in the Tidewater
Virginia metropolitan region, producing at least
seven plays and musicals a season for 14 consecutive summers.

As a general rule, however, you will not want to emphasize your dates. Place them within the entry either after the lead, in the text of the entry, or at the end of the entry as follows:

Date After Lead:

Employment: <u>**Artistic Director,**</u> Norfolk Theater Festival,
1974–87. Planned, organized, and managed the
most popular theater series in the Tidewater
Virginia metropolitan region, producing at least
seven plays and musicals a season for 14 consecutive summers.

Date Within Entry:

Employment: <u>**Norfolk Theater Festival.**</u> Artistic Director.
From 1974 to 1987, planned, organized, and
managed the most popular theater series in the
Tidewater Virginia metropolitan region, producing
at least seven plays and musicals a season for 14
consecutive summers.

Date at the End of the Entry:

Employment: <u>**Artistic Director,**</u> Norfolk Theater Festival.
Planned, organized, and managed the most
popular theater series in the Tidewater Virginia
metropolitan region, producing at least seven plays
and musicals a season for 14 consecutive summers. 1974–87.

To summarize, then, you should highlight dates in the left margin or as leads if the dates themselves are the strong points.

Otherwise, to hide or to downplay your irrelevant dates, place them after the lead, within the entry, or at the end of the entry.

How to Display Dates

Read this quickly. Then look away from the page and see if you can remember the dates when this person was employed: 6/10/89–9/27/89, 6/14/90–9/12/90, 5/6/91–7/11/91. Now look away real fast. Can you remember the dates? Wasn't it irritating trying to figure out the months, days, and years? Now read this quickly and you'll immediately remember when this person was employed: Summers 1989, 1990, 1991.

The bottom line? Don't use numerals and slashes to reveal dates. Instead, spell out the time period such as summer, spring, Christmas break, or whatever. Or to give beginning and ending dates of a longer-term job, either give the beginning and ending years (1989–91) or spell out the beginning month and year and the ending month and year, like this: November 1989–June 1991. That's a lot more comprehensible and pleasing to the eye than 11/3/89–6/6/91.

You're about ready to begin writing your resume.

But first, write this way, folks!

CHAPTER 5

Write This Way, Folks!

Rules for Grammar and Style

EMPLOYERS WANT PEOPLE WITH well-developed communication skills. Certainly your ability to write might interest the employer. Your resume is a written document, and should thus serve as a sample of your writing skill. Yet many people will prepare a resume chock full of grammatical mistakes, written in a style that would make a grammar school English teacher cringe. Let's look carefully at the writing style you should use as well as some of the grammatical mistakes people often make.

Resume Talk: Listings

Resume information will appear either as listings or sentences. If a group of words has a verb in it, it's a sentence. If it has no verb, it's a listing. Here is an example of a listing: "B.A. in History, May 1985." Here's an example of a sentence: "Worked forty hours per week waiting tables, assisting in the kitchen, and responding personally to customers."

The only real problem presented by listings is punctuation. Does a listing end with a period? The answer is maybe yes, maybe no. If a listing is followed by a sentence or another listing on the same line, it should end with a period. Study this example:

> B.A. in History, May 1985. Curriculum included a broad array of liberal arts courses requiring extensive writing.

Because that listing was followed by a sentence on the same line, a period obviously was needed to end the listing. But take a look at this example:

> University of North Carolina, Chapel Hill, NC
> B.A. in History, May 1985

Both of those lines are listings not followed by other words on the same line. Thus, no period is necessary. You could, however, decide to include periods at the end of the listings, and it would be perfectly okay. The goal is consistency. As you create your resume, make certain that if one listing has no period, all listings have no periods. Also, of course, make certain all resume sentences do end with periods.

Resume Talk: Sentences

Most of your resume information will appear in sentences because you are writing your message for your audience to show your accomplishments. To do this you must use verbs. If you use verbs, you're writing sentences. The resume sentence is different from the sentences you're used to constructing. To avoid overusing the first-person pronoun *I* as the subject of sentences, the resume sentence drops the grammatical subject. Thus, do not write, "I developed a new inventory system saving 25% of floor space." Instead write, "Developed a new inventory system saving 25% of floor space."

There is, however, no absolute prohibition on use of first-person pronouns. We've seen some very effective resumes that included an occasional *I, me, my,* or *mine.* They result in highly personal documents quite appealing in style and tone. As an example, here is the objective of a friend of ours who is seeking a position in accounting:

Objective: After completing a rigorous liberal arts curriculum at Mary Baldwin College, while simultaneously working on an Associates in Applied Science in Accounting at Piedmont Virginia Community College, I have decided to obtain a position that will benefit from and enhance my accounting background.

Also, sometimes you must use first-person pronouns to emphasize a point. For example, suppose you held the same summer job for three summers. You correctly decide to emphasize that you were asked to return for two additional summers, and want to use that verb *asked*. You've got to put it in either active or passive voice, but whichever voice you choose you cannot strongly make your point without using a first-person pronoun. If you choose the active voice, there's no way you can write the sentence without using the first-person pronoun *me*. You have to write, "The manager asked me to return for two additional summers." If you use the passive voice, you can write the sentence without using a first-person pronoun, but you end up with a weak point: "Asked to return for two additional summers," or, "Was asked to return for two additional summers." Using the first-person pronoun yields this: "I was asked to return for two additional summers."

Finally, as we've mentioned before, put your verbs in the first person, not the third person. We have seen some resumes that use the third person, like this: "Delegates tasks to staff members, orders all supplies, and is responsible for balancing daily receipts." This resume sounds like it's talking about somebody other than the resume writer.

Grammatical Mistakes

It is unfortunate, but many resume writers make significant grammatical mistakes when composing their resumes. Nothing could be worse, of course, than touting one's communication skills with grammatically incorrect prose. Without producing a complete grammar book here, we do feel compelled to review the most common mistakes people make.

Nonparallel Construction

The grammatical mistake most frequently appearing on resumes is nonparallel construction. Whenever you state a series of things, you must use the same grammatical construction for each element of the series. To use a simple example, don't write, "Yesterday, I went boating, hiking, and took a bicycle ride." Once you adopt the gerund for the first element of the series, *hiking*, you must follow the same grammatical construction for all elements of the series. Thus, "Yesterday, I went boating, hiking, and cycling."

In a resume, the writer frequently must reveal a series of events, duties, entities, or accomplishments, so the odds of writing a nonparallel construction are quite high. Thus, we've seen nonparallel constructions like this: "Developed new inventory control system that saved limited space, expedited orders, and cost saving of $500 per month." Once you begin that listing of verbs of the dependent clause ("saved limited space, expedited orders"), each item on the list must be a verb of the dependent clause. Thus: "Developed new inventory control system that saved limited space, expedited orders, and cut costs by $500 per month."

Verb Tense

Verb tense sometimes presents a problem. If you're describing a previous job or activity, then definitely use the past tense. If you're describing your current position or activities, use the present tense, even though this will require you to revise your resume as soon as that current job or activity ceases.

Capitalization

Each resume sentence should begin with a capital letter. Each resume listing appearing on a line by itself or following a period on the same line should begin with a capital letter. Thus, don't do this:

Education: <u>University of Virginia</u>, Charlottesville, Virginia
B.A. in History, May 1985
coursework in computers and marketing
honors included Dean's List & Departmental
Honors

In the above example the coursework is listed on a line by itself. It should begin with a capital letter. The honors line is a resume sentence, which should begin with a capital letter as well. The resume sentence also should end with a period, although the other listings in that entry need not end with periods.

Avoid seemingly clever tricks, like typing your name in lowercase letters. Also, any resume listing or parts of a resume sentence following a comma or a semicolon should begin with a lowercase letter. This is a common mistake. Many writers for some reason will produce this:

Duties included Taking inventory; Meeting customers; Ordering stock; Operating the cash register.

Follow ordinary, grammatical rules of capitalization.

Abbreviations

The only permissible abbreviations in a resume are abbreviated street addresses, abbreviated states, and well-known acronyms. Abbreviations don't look very good, so whenever possible, don't abbreviate street addresses or states at all. If you abbreviate a state in one place in the resume, make certain all states are abbreviated. Also, for the fifty states use the two-letter abbreviations currently accepted by the Post Office. The following are a list of abbreviations.

Alabama (AL)

Alaska (AK)

Arizona (AZ)

Arkansas (AR)

California (CA)

Colorado (CO)

Connecticut (CT)

Delaware (DE)

District of Columbia (DC)

Florida (FL)

Georgia (GA)

Hawaii (HI)

Idaho (ID)

Illinois (IL)

Indiana (IN)

Iowa (IA)

Kansas (KS)

Kentucky (KY)

Louisiana (LA)

Maine (ME)

Maryland (MD)

Massachusetts (MA)

Michigan (MI)

Minnesota (MN)

Mississippi (MS)

Missouri (MO)

Missouri (MO)

Montana (MT)

Nebraska (NE)

Nevada (NV)

New Hamp shire (NH)

New Jersey (NJ)

New Mexico (NM)

New York (NY)

North Carolina (NC)

North Dakota (ND)

Ohio (OH)

Oklahoma (OK)

Oregon (OR)

Pennsylvania (PA)

Rhode Island (RI)

South Carolina (SC)

South Dakota (SD)

Tennessee (TN)

Texas (TX)

Utah (UT)

Vermont (VT)

Virginia (VA)

Washington (WA)

West Virginia (WV)

Wisconsin (WI)

Wyoming (WY)

Avoid almost all other abbreviations. Do not write the Department of Transportation as Dept. of Transportation or Dep't of Transportation. Do not put your position as Ass't Manager, or worse, Ass't Mgr. Write those words out; they look awful when abbreviated.

Perhaps the only other acceptable abbreviation is a widely known acronym. Thus, the Atlantic Coast Conference is the

ACC. The National Collegiate Athletic Association is the NCAA. The National Association for the Advancement of Colored People is the NAACP. The same would hold true for most federal agencies. The National Labor Relations Board is the NLRB. The Securities and Exchange Commission is the SEC. But unless the acronym is a household word, don't use it.

Matters of Style

One of the best ways to write powerfully is to use action verbs. If you use too many nouns, your writing will be mushy, weak, and ineffective. Read this and you'll see what I mean:

> Responsibilities as Assistant Manager included development and implementation of a new inventory system with a result of a maximization of space utilization.

That sounds like a page from a Pentagon standard operating procedure manual. Notice the nouns: development, implementation, result, maximization, and utilization. They're weak, mushy, and limp. Instead, you can convert many of those nouns to verbs and zap others to produce this:

> As Assistant Manager, developed and implemented a new inventory system that saved considerable space.

Now you've said the same thing using fewer words. The revised passage clips along, insisting that the reader pay attention. It has power and action. The reason? Verbs.

You want to avoid mushy noun-speak. To develop the knack you should watch carefully for a special kind of noun, the derivative noun. A derivative noun is derived from a verb, such as conclusion, implementation, emphasis, inference, and the list could go on forever. Watch for the suffixes *-tion, -sion, -ence, -ance, -ency,* and *-ancy.* These typically are used to convert a verb into a noun.

Think about it for a minute. What part of speech is absolutely necessary to write an English sentence? A noun? Nope. A verb. Suppose you choose a derivative noun to convey a verb meaning. You still need a verb to complete the sentence. So you grope around for another verb to hang the derivative noun on. Thus, you say things like this: "The board reached the decision that . . . ." You chose the derivative noun *decision* and then groped for the verb *reached*. The problem disappears if you convert *decision* to its verb form *decide*: "The board decided . . . ."

This one simple trick of declaring war on derivative nouns and converting them to their base verbs will tighten up your writing considerably. You'll be more persuasive, you'll use fewer words, and your writing will be action-packed. And if you're writing a thirty-second advertisement for yourself, that's what you want to be: persuasive and concise.

Writing with action verbs is so important that we developed a list of verbs that relate directly to resume writing. Study this list, which appears in the Appendix. Check those verbs that describe your life, your education, your employment, your activities, your interests, and your accomplishments. You'll be well on your way to writing a potent and convincing resume.

"Responsible for" and "Duties included"

A final word on verbs. To write with verbs you want to avoid nouns. Watch out for two overused expressions in resumes that require you to use noun forms. First, avoid the expression "Duties included," which requires a noun or series of nouns to complete the sentence. You'd have to write, "Duties included management of cash drawer, supervision of eight other employees, and creation of all advertisements." By zapping "Duties included" and converting derivative nouns to verbs, you write, "Managed the cash drawer, supervised eight other employees, and created all advertisements." Second, avoid the expression, "Responsible for." Notice you're setting up a prepositional phrase, which requires a noun or series of nouns to complete the phrase. To complete the sentence you would have to write, "Responsible for management of cash drawer, supervision of eight other employees, and creation of all advertisements." By avoiding "Responsible for" and writing with verbs, you obliterate the problem of weak nouns.

Sometimes, of course, you cannot avoid "Responsible for" or "Duties included." If you need to use either, then choose gerunds as noun forms to complete the expressions. Thus, "Responsible for managing cash drawer, supervising eight other employees, and creating all advertisements."

Tooting Your Horn with Adjectives and Adverbs

Throughout this book we emphasize the importance of tooting your own horn. No one else will toot it for you. You have to do it. One good way to congratulate yourself is with adjectives and adverbs. When describing an accomplishment, don't just say you "completed all assignments." Instead say that you "successfully completed all assignments on time." Don't say you "were assigned the task of entering the names and addresses of 20,000 businesses." Instead write, "Tackled the enormous task of entering the names and addresses of 20,000 businesses."

Learning to toot your horn is so important in resume writing, we've prepared a list of adjectives and adverbs. It appears in Appendix A. Study it carefully. Find evidence of you. Remember the sixteen attributes the employer wants, and toot away!

Using Numbers

Why is baseball the national pastime? Why is The Count the most popular character on "Sesame Street"? Why do the headlines in the daily newspaper inevitably reveal yet another poll? Because Americans love numbers. We thrive on statistics. We itch to quantify everything. You should love numbers, too. Right in your resume. As you describe your accomplishments, include healthy doses of numbers that favor you. Thus, don't say you "served as Kitchen Manager of Zeta, Zeta, Zeta." Instead say you "served as Kitchen Manager of Zeta, Zeta, Zeta and successfully controlled an annual budget of $85,000." Don't say you "recruited and trained the sales force serving the southeast region." Instead, say you "recruited and trained a sales force of twenty-eight people serving twelve states in the southeast region and producing $3.4 million in annual sales."

When you use numbers to describe your accomplishments, be sure the numbers are strong numbers, not weak numbers. Here's an example of a weak number: "As Assistant Bank Teller, controlled a daily cash drawer with a $1,000 limit." Make the numbers favor you. If you can, turn a weak number into a strong number. Using the same bank teller example, calculate the total amount of cash that passed through your hands during the job and write, "As Assistant Bank Teller, controlled a cash drawer and successfully accounted for more than $250,000 in cash."

So Much for Content and Style

When you combine what you've learned about content in Chapter 4 with what you learned about style in this chapter, you're ready to put your resume on paper. By following the instructions on content and style you can produce a terrific resume. But that terrific, well-built resume might very well be a loser. Its format might be awful. Its paper might be a bit weird. Content and writing style are not enough. You must pay careful attention to appearance. Otherwise your well-written, carefully structured resume might still end up in the reject pile.

CHAPTER 6

Balloons and Dancing Bears

Resume Formatting

COLLEAGUES WHO GREW UP in the 1960s will recall the fashion of collectively sneering at fashion and most every other norm. We can remember fashionably thinking that no one should be allowed to judge us by the clothes we wear. After all, we figured, if they can't see our intrinsic value, that's their problem, not ours. Over time, people began to whistle a different tune. Books like *Dress for Success* began to appear. Experts in body language emerged. An entire industry of images boomed. The children of the '60s got caught with their ratty old pants down, but the next generation tuned into the importance of images. They realized that people do judge other people, at least initially, by what they wear. Even our generation had to admit that first impressions make a vital difference. We began to realize a fact of reality: You never get a second chance to make a first impression!

First Impressions: Sizing People Up

Picture this. You're nervously waiting to interview a recruiter. The time arrives, and you're ushered into the room. You immediately size up the interviewer. How? By only two senses: what you see and what you hear. What do you see? Well, you don't see much skin, do you? Just a face and some hands sticking out of a suit coat. You see size: tall, short, fat, or thin. But what is your main visual image? Much of what you see during the first thirty seconds is clothing. Of course, the recruiter is sizing you up, too. What is one of the first things the recruiter sees? Clothes. This chapter is not about proper dress in an interview, but rather the clothing on your resume. Which will it be? Blue jeans? Or a navy blue suit?

First Impressions: Sizing Up Your Resume

Remember that employment manager facing a stack of eighty resumes to review each day. She takes a thirty-second scan. She's sizing you up, and initially she sees only the appearance of your resume—format and paper. She can't see your tight and action-packed writing style, or even your credentials, not initially. All she sees at first is the clothing on your resume. And that first, quick glance produces a reaction that might well determine whether she listens to your pitch or tunes you out, banishing you forever to the reject pile.

The Importance of Formatting

This chapter is about your resume's clothing, its format and layout. If your resume wears blue jeans, that's the first impression the employment manager will have of you. If your resume is messy, that's what the employment manager thinks of you. If your resume has a weird format, the employment manager probably thinks you have a weird format. You will never have a second chance to make this first, vital impression. You might have written the world's best resume and not get a single interview. You have the world's best toothpaste, but nobody's buying. Unfortunately, you've put it in an unattractive package.

To produce a winning resume you must pay careful attention to its format. In short, you must package yourself professionally by producing a tasteful but powerful advertisement.

Balloons and Dancing Bears

Think of the tasteful and memorable commercials you've seen on TV. They're the ones that succeed in getting the attention of people with good taste. Then think of the car dealer ads, the ones with balloons, trumpets, tubas, cheerleaders, confetti, clowns, dogs, screaming salespeople, and dancing bears. Those ads are overemphasized. By emphasizing all messages, they emphasize none. Those ads might appeal to people with no taste, but they don't impress people with good taste, which we assume includes the employment managers and other hiring executives of this world.

Many resume writers come up with the most tortured formats imaginable. The reason, we think, is that many people feel compelled to draw the reader's eye to every fact found in the resume. They feel they have to set everything off to make everything stand out. They format the written word like it would never be formatted anywhere else—not in a book, thesis, or dissertation, not on a poster, and certainly not in any decently formatted advertisement. Seeking to make everything stand out, many resumes resemble the used-car ads, complete with balloons and dancing bears:

Education: 9/90–6/94, B.A. Economics, University of North Carolina

    courses included: • Microeconomics
             • Macroeconomics
             • Money & Banking
             • Economic Statistics

  Activities: – Order of the Old Well
       – Yackety Yack Yearbook Staff
       – The Daily Tarheel Sports Section

Cumulative Grade Point Average: 3.5 overall
               3.8 in major

The problem with that mess is that nothing stands out, except maybe the bulging eyes of the employment manager as she strains to bring order out of chaos. Take a look at it. It has six separate left-hand margins: (1) far left at the Education heading; (2) at the beginning of the lead; (3) at the word *courses*; (4) at the word *Microeconomics*; (5) at the word *Order*; and (6) at the numeral *3.5*. And what determined those margins? Nothing more than the fortuity of the length of certain subheadings and a desire to set everything off so it'll stand out.

When you sit down to put together your resume, you face two problems of formatting. First, you must decide what goes where, or the graphics of positioning. The graphics of positioning will determine the overall layout of your resume. Second, once you've chosen an overall layout, you must decide on the graphics of emphasis to make things stand out. By carefully and tastefully choosing the correct graphics of positioning and emphasis, you'll avoid the balloons and dancing bears syndrome, the death knell of most resumes.

The Graphics of Positioning

What goes where? The graphics of positioning determines the overall appearance of your resume. You must decide on the actual placement of your caption and your headings. Then you must create a consistent way to display your entries. Let's study each in turn.

One-Address Caption

If you have a one-address caption, you may either center it or put it to the far left margin. In the centered caption, be careful with your city and state, however. If your city and state have a large number of characters, you should abbreviate the state to the two-letter postal abbreviation. Otherwise, you'll end up with something like this:

JAMES SMITH
401 Main St.
Chattanooga, Tennessee 33333
(401) 999-9991

The city and state line takes up so much room, the caption doesn't look good. You should abbreviate the state to produce this:

JAMES SMITH
401 Main Street
Chattanooga, TN 33333
(401) 999-9991

The trick for centered captions is to make the length of each line match the others as closely as possible. In the above example, we abbreviated *Tennessee* and spelled out the word *Street* to make the lengths of the lines as close to equal as possible.

The same considerations hold for the left-margin, one-address caption. Take a look at the same two examples:

JAMES SMITH
401 Main St.
Chattanooga, Tennessee 33333
(401) 999-9991

JAMES SMITH
401 Main Street
Chattanooga, TN 33333
(401) 999-9991

In the second example, making the lines as close to equal length as possible produces a more pleasing format.

Two-Address Caption

The two-address caption will show your home address or permanent address and your present (temporary) address, school address, or office address. Again, center your name at the top. Then select the address that has the longest address lines to put at the left and the address with the shortest address lines at the right. Here's why:

JAMES SMITH

Home Address:	School Address:
401 Jefferson	1243 Devonshire Lane
Mapp, Ohio 23333	Apartment No. 2
(203) 974-7836	Chattanooga, Tennessee 33333
	(401) 999-9991

The above format is unbalanced to the right. You can solve this problem by putting the longest address, here the school address, at the left margin, by abbreviating *Tennessee*, and by getting rid of *Apartment No.* Try this:

JAMES SMITH

School Address:	Home Address:
1243 Devonshire Lane No. 2	401 Jefferson
Chattanooga, TN 33333	Mapp, Ohio 23333
(401) 999-9991	(203) 974-7836

Caption Creativity

The two formats above for the one-address and two-address captions are not chiseled in stone. There is room for creativity. But watch out. Be creative if you truly have skill in the graphic arts. Otherwise, you'll end up producing something that'll only hurt your chances for an interview. We've seen some effective variations on formatting the caption. Here's a sample of a different one-address caption that saved considerable vertical space for a writer who wanted a one-page resume:

JAMES SMITH 1243 Devonshire Lane, Mapp, Ohio 23333 (203) 974-7836

And here's a one-address caption of a writer who wanted to emphasize her place and date of birth. She effectively pulled it off by using a two-address format:

JANE SMITH

1243 Devonshire Lane	Born January 2, 1958 in
Mapp, Ohio 23333	Ft. Lauderdale, Florida
(203) 974-7836	

Don't hesitate to be creative, but resist the temptation to be bizarre.

Headings

Formatting the headings will determine the overall appearance and perhaps even the length of your resume. Two basic possibilities exist: left-margin headings and centered headings. Let's look at each basic type on the following two pages. (To illustrate the formatting techniques that follow, we have provided some mock sample resumes, using meaningless characters to display the format. This way you can pay attention to the format only and not get sidetracked actually reading sample resume text.)

Centered Headings: A Word of Caution. You might think the centered-heading format allows you to get more information on your resume. This is probably true if you have a great deal of text and relatively few headings. But if you have quite a few headings, the centered-heading format actually will reduce the amount of space available for text. The heading in a centered-heading format takes up three lines: one above the heading, one for the heading, and one below the heading. Thus, if you have a resume with six headings, the centered-heading format eats up eighteen lines just for the headings alone.

Furthermore, unless you have a lot of text and relatively few headings, the centered-heading format doesn't look very good. This is especially evident when you keep in mind that the lines in each entry will be of varying length. The headings, therefore, will tend to get lost. The overall visual effect will be out of balance, due primarily to the small amount of text and the varying length of the lines in each entry. Thus, unless you have lots of text and relatively few headings, you should probably use the left-margin format.

Left-Margin Headings: The Margin for Entries. In the left-margin heading format, the headings appear at the far left margin. The entries then should appear in the next established margin. They

Basic Left-Margin Heading Format

JAMES SMITH
1401 Main Avenue
Richmond, VA 22222
(804) 999-9998

Objective: xxxxxxxxxxxxxxxxxxxxxxxxxxxxxxxxxxxxxxx
xxxxxxxxxxxxxxxxxxxxxxxxxxxxxxxxxxxxxxx
xxxxxxxxxxxxxxxxxxxxxxxxxxxxxxxxxxxxxxx

Education: xxxxxxxxxxxxxxxxxxxxxxxxxxxxxxxxxxxxxxx
xxxxxxxxxxxxxxxxxxxxxxxxxxxxxxxxxxxxxxx
xxxxxxxxxxxxxxxxxxxxxxxxxxxxxxxxxxxxxxx
xxxxxxxxxxxxxxxxxxxxxxxxxxxxxxxxxxxxxxx
xxxxxxxxxxxxxxxxxxxxxxxxxxxxxxxxxxxxxxx

xxxxxxxxxxxxxxxxxxxxxxxxxxxxxxxxxxxxxxx
xxxxxxxxxxxxxxxxxxxxxxxxxxxxxxxxxxxxxxx
xxxxxxxxxxxxxxxxxxxxxxxxxxxxxxxxxxxxxxx

Employment: xxxxxxxxxxxxxxxxxxxxxxxxxxxxxxxxxxxxxxx
xxxxxxxxxxxxxxxxxxxxxxxxxxxxxxxxxxxxxxx
xxxxxxxxxxxxxxxxxxxxxxxxxxxxxxxxxxxxxxx
xxxxxxxxxxxxxxxxxxxxxxxxxxxxxxxxxxxxxxx
xxxxxxxxxxxxxxxxxxxxxxxxxxxxxxxxxxxxxxx
xxxxxxxxxxxxxxxxxxxxxxxxxxxxxxxxxxxxxxx

xxxxxxxxxxxxxxxxxxxxxxxxxxxxxxxxxxxxxxx
xxxxxxxxxxxxxxxxxxxxxxxxxxxxxxxxxxxxxxx

xxxxxxxxxxxxxxxxxxxxxxxxxxxxxxxxxxxxxxx
xxxxxxxxxxxxxxxxxxxxxxxxxxxxxxxxxxxxxxx

Activities: xxxxxxxxxxxxxxxxxxxxxxxxxxxxxxxxxxxxxxx
xxxxxxxxxxxxxxxxxxxxxxxxxxxxxxxxxxxxxxx
xxxxxxxxxxxxxxxxxxxxxxxxxxxxxxxxxxxxxxx
xxxxxxxxxxxxxxxxxxxxxxxxxxxxxxxxxxxxxxx

References: Excellent references will be provided on request.

Basic Centered-Heading Format

JAMES SMITH
1401 Main Avenue
Richmond, VA 22222
(804) 999-9998

OBJECTIVE

xxxxxxxxxxxxxxxxxxxxxxxxxxxxxxxxxxxxxxxxxxxxxxxxxxxxxxx
xxxxxxxxxxxxxxxxxxxxxxxxxxxxxxxxxxxxxxxxxxxxxxxxxxxxxxx

EDUCATION

xxxxxxxxxxxxxxxxxxxxxxxxxxxxxxxxxxxxxxxxxxxxxxxxxxxxxxx
xxxxxxxxxxxxxxxxxxxxxxxxxxxxxxxxxxxxxxxxxxxxxxxxxxxxxxx

xxxxxxxxxxxxxxxxxxxxxxxxxxxxxxxxxxxxxxxxxxxxxxxxxxxxxxx
xxxxxxxxxxxxxxxxxxxxxxxxxxxxxxxxxxxxxxxxxxxxxxxxxxxxxxx
xxxxxxxxxxxxxxxxxxxxxxxxxxxxxxxxxxxxxxxxxxxxxxxxxxxxxxx

EMPLOYMENT

xxxxxxxxxxxxxxxxxxxxxxxxxxxxxxxxxxxxxxxxxxxxxxxxxxxxxxx
xxxxxxxxxxxxxxxxxxxxxxxxxxxxxxxxxxxxxxxxxxxxxxxxxxxxxxx
xxxxxxxxxxxxxxxxxxxxxxxxxxxxxxxxxxxxxxxxxxxxxxxxxxxxxxx

xxxxxxxxxxxxxxxxxxxxxxxxxxxxxxxxxxxxxxxxxxxxxxxxxxxxxxx
xxxxxxxxxxxxxxxxxxxxxxxxxxxxxxxxxxxxxxxxxxxxxxxxxxxxxxx
xxxxxxxxxxxxxxxxxxxxxxxxxxxxxxxxxxxxxxxxxxxxxxxxxxxxxxx

xxxxxxxxxxxxxxxxxxxxxxxxxxxxxxxxxxxxxxxxxxxxxxxxxxxxxxx
xxxxxxxxxxxxxxxxxxxxxxxxxxxxxxxxxxxxxxxxxxxxxxxxxxxxxxx
xxxxxxxxxxxxxxxxxxxxxxxxxxxxxxxxxxxxxxxxxxxxxxxxxxxxxxx

ACTIVITIES

xxxxxxxxxxxxxxxxxxxxxxxxxxxxxxxxxxxxxxxxxxxxxxxxxxxxxx
xxxxxxxxxxxxxxxxxxxxxxxxxxxxxxxxxxxxxxxxxxxxxxxxxxxxxx
xxxxxxxxxxxxxxxxxxxxxxxxxxxxxxxxxxxxxxxxxxxxxxxxxxxxxx

Professional References Provided On Request

should not have a varying margin depending on the length of the heading. For example, do not create multiple margins like this:

Education: xxxxxxxxxxxxxxxxxxxxxxxxxxxxxxxxxxxxxxxxxx
             xxxxxxxxxxxxxxxxxxxxxxxxxxxxxxxxxxxxxxxxx
Computer Experience: xxxxxxxxxxxxxxxxxxxxxxxxxxxxxxxx
             xxxxxxxxxxxxxxxxxxxxxxxxxxxxxxxxxxxx
             xxxxxxxxxxxxxxxxxxxxxxxxxxxxxxxxxx

Instead, all entries should appear flush to the margin that you determine—one margin, not multiple margins. So if you adopt the left-margin heading format, be very careful about determining the left margin for your entries. Many people make terrible mistakes by letting the length of headings determine the margin for entries. Let's use a ridiculous example to illustrate the point:

JAMES SMITH
1401 Main Avenue
Richmond, VA 22222
(804) 999-9998

Summary of Qualifications: xxxxxxxxxxxxxxxxxxxxxxxxxxxxxxx
Education: xxxxxxxxxxxxxxxxxxxxxxxxxxxxxxx
                            xxxxxxxxxxxxxxxxxxxxxxxxxxxxx
Employment: xxxxxxxxxxxxxxxxxxxxxxxxxxxxx
                            xxxxxxxxxxxxxxxxxxxxxxxxxxxxx
                            xxxxxxxxxxxxxxxxxxxxxxxxxxxxx

That format leans too far to the right. The problem arose because the margin was determined by the length of a heading rather than by considerations of graphic art. The heading should not set the margin, you should. So follow this cardinal rule of formatting: Never let the length of your heading determine a margin for your entries.

Dealing with Long Headings.   If you have a long heading, there are three simple cures: (1) rename the heading; (2) stack the heading; or (3) leave the heading on a line by itself. Here are three solutions to the problem presented by the example above.

Rename the heading:

Summary: xxxxxxxxxxxxxxxxxxxxxxxxxxxxxxxxxxxxxxxxxxx
            xxxxxxxxxxxxxxxxxxxxxxxxxxxxxxxxxxxxxxxxx

Stack the heading:

Summary of   xxxxxxxxxxxxxxxxxxxxxxxxxxxxxxxxxxxxxxxxxx
Qualifications: xxxxxxxxxxxxxxxxxxxxxxxxxxxxxxxxxxxxxxxxx

Leave the heading on a line by itself:

Summary of Qualifications:

            xxxxxxxxxxxxxxxxxxxxxxxxxxxxxxxxxxxxxxxxxxxxx
            xxxxxxxxxxxxxxxxxxxxxxxxxxxxxxxxxxxxxxxxxxxxx

In the second example, notice that you begin the entry on the first line of the multiline heading. Do not put the first entry line on the last line of the multiline heading; otherwise, you'll have uneven amounts of space between stacked and unstacked headings on your resume. In the third example, begin the entry at the margin you have chosen. To set off the entry you may drop down two lines, as we have done.

There are many variations on these two basic formats. In Chapter 8 we will provide eight basic formats of the same resume so that you can obtain some ideas for creating your own.

Consistent Appearance of Entries

Multiple margins and indentations present similar problems in resume entries. As you format your entries, keep in mind that a margin or indentation tends to attract the reader's eye. If too many margins and too many indentations try to attract the reader's eye, you'll end up with the mess we saw earlier. Here it is again:

Education: 9/90–6/94, B.A. Economics, University of
North Carolina

courses included: • Microeconomics
• Macroeconomics
• Money & Banking
• Economic Statistics

Activities: – Order of the Old Well
– Yackety Yack Yearbook Staff
– The Daily Tarheel Sports Section

Cumulative Grade Point Average: 3.5 overall
3.8 in major

The trick in repairing that resume entry is to write and format it the way all other written information is prepared: in neat, crisp paragraphs or lists. By writing as we ordinarily write and playing a few graphic tricks of emphasis (discussed below), we can produce this:

Education: **UNDERLINE UNIVERSITY OF NORTH CAROLINA,** Chapel Hill, NC
B.A. Economics, May 1984. Courses included Microeconomics, Macroeconomics, Money & Banking, and Economic Statistics.

Activities: Order of the Old Well, Yackety Yack Yearbook Staff, The Daily Tarheel Sports Section.

Cumulative GPA = 3.5 overall; 3.8 in major.

That looks like what most people are accustomed to reading: paragraphs. To achieve this look, remember two rules: (1) don't let the length of words determine margins or indentations; (2) don't have more than two or three indentations in the entire resume.

The types of mistakes people make in formatting resume entries are fairly predictable. At the top of the list is multiple margins. Here's an example where the writer succumbed to the temptation to make everything stand out and produced an awkward-looking format:

Education: World University, Plains, Montana.
B.A. History expected June 1994.

Honors: xxxxxxxxxxxxxxxxxxxxxxxxxxxxxxxxxxxxxxxxxxxxxxx
xxxxxxxxxxxxxxxxxxxxxxxxxxxxxxxxxxxxxxxxxxxxxx
xxxxxxxxxxxxxxxxxxxxxxxxxxxxxxxxxxxxxxxxxx

Activities: xxxxxxxxxxxxxxxxxxxxxxxxxxxxxxxxxxxxxxxxxxxxxxx
xxxxxxxxxxxxxxxxxxxxxxxxxxxxxxxxxxxxxxxxxxxxxxxx
xxxxxxxxxxxxxxxxxxxxxxxxxxxxxxxxxxxxxxxxxxxxxx

This format shows four distinct margins. Nowhere else is the written word presented this way. Neither should your words appear this way in your most important document, your resume. Instead, you could adopt the paragraph format and reformat this resume like this:

Education: **WORLD UNIVERSITY**, Plains, Montana.
B.A. History expected June 1994.

Honors: xxxxxxxxxxxxxxxxxxxxxxxxxxxxxxxxxxxxxxxxxxxxxxx
xxxxxxxxxxxxxxxxxxxxxxxxxxxxxxxxxxxxxxxxxxxxxx

Activities: xxxxxxxxxxxxxxxxxxxxxxxxxxxxxxxxxxxxxxxxxxxxxxx
xxxxxxxxxxxxxxxxxxxxxxxxxxxxxxxxxxxxxxxxxxxxxx

If you firmly believe multiple margins are needed to make things stand out, then try to use as few as possible. Be sure to follow the same formatting approach for all entries, and make certain you determine the margins. Don't let the fortuity of subheading length make those decisions. This resume, then, could appear like this:

Education: **WORLD UNIVERSITY**, Plains, Montana.
B.A. History expected June 1994.

Honors: xxxxxxxxxxxxxxxxxxxxxxxxxxxxxxxxxx
xxxxxxxxxxxxxxxxxxxxxxxxxxxxxxxxxxxxxxx
xxxxxxxxxxxxxxxxxxxxxxxxxxxxxxxxxxxxx

Activities: xxxxxxxxxxxxxxxxxxxxxxxxxxxxxxxx
xxxxxxxxxxxxxxxxxxxxxxxxxxxxxxxxxxxx
xxxxxxxxxxxxxxxxxxxxxxxxxxxxxxxxxxxxxxx

The Graphics of Positioning: A Summary

The overall layout of your resume determines the reader's first reaction. The layout should be neat and professional. Your headings should be centered or placed at the left margin. Your entries should appear as blocked paragraphs that line up along a single margin. If you wish to emphasize certain parts of your entries by indenting beyond the established entry margin, make sure a sense of aesthetics governs your choice of margins. Also make sure indentations appearing in one entry are repeated consistently in other entries. Graphically, you are trying to force the reader's eye to your strongest points. Keep your strategies consistent. Don't keep changing the graphic rules on the reader.

Having created the overall layout of your resume, you can now turn your attention to the all-important devices you can use to emphasize your strengths, the graphics of emphasis.

The Graphics of Emphasis

Now we get to the real tricks of the trade. When the employment manager gives your resume that thirty-second scan, you want to control the eyes of the beholder so that she will see the beauty in you. You do so by using one or more of the following seven techniques of graphic emphasis:

1. CAPITALIZATION
2. <u>Underlining</u>
3. **Bold**
4. *Italics*
5. Vertical Spacing
6. Horizontal Spacing
7. Punctuation

Caps, Underlining, Bold, and Italics

You should use the first four—capitalization, underlining, bold, and italics—to accentuate your name, your strongest leads, important information within entries, and maybe your headings. Choosing the right mix and extent of graphic emphasis is the trick. You don't want to overdo it, or the emphasis loses its impact. You should keep in mind, for example, that if you emphasize some leads, you don't have to emphasize all leads. You emphasize only those few messages you want to force the reader's eye to see.

The following examples use a variety of the first four graphic devices. Notice the permutations are virtually endless.

Education: **University of North Carolina,** Chapel Hill, NC
B.A. in History, May 1994. Curriculum included more than 33 hours in pre-med courses. GPA = 3.85 on a 4.0 scale.

Education: University of North Carolina, Chapel Hill, NC
B.A. in History, May 1994. Curriculum included more than 33 hours in pre-med courses. GPA = 3.85 on a 4.0 scale.

Education: **University of North Carolina,** Chapel Hill, NC
B.A. in History, May 1994. Curriculum included more than 33 hours in pre-med courses. *GPA = 3.85 on a 4.0 scale.*

Education: **UNIVERSITY OF NORTH CAROLINA,** Chapel Hill, NC
B.A. in History, May 1994. Curriculum included more than 33 hours in pre-med courses. **GPA = 3.85 on a 4.0 scale.**

Vertical and Horizontal Spacing

You should use the next two, vertical and horizontal spacing, to make parts of an entry stand out. For example, instead of multiple margins, use vertical spacing and drop down two lines to set off the point or experience you're extolling. Here's an example of emphasis by vertical spacing that sets apart the honors information:

Education: <u>**UNIVERSITY OF NORTH CAROLINA,**</u> Chapel Hill, NC
B.A. in History, May 1994. Curriculum included
more than 33 hours in pre-med courses. GPA = 3.6
on a 4.0 scale.
Honors: Order of the Old Well, Order of the Grail
(both recognizing outstanding contributions to
university life).

Horizontal spacing can be used to pull some information over to the extreme right-hand margin to set it off. For example, if you include the date on the lead line, you might want to emphasize the date this way:

Employment: <u>**Acme, Inc.,**</u> Charleston, SC   Summer 1984

xxxxxxxxxxxxxxxxxxxxxxxxxxxxxxxxxxxxxxxxx
xxxxxxxxxxxxxxxxxxxxxxxxxxxxxxxxxxxxxxxxx
xxxxxxxxxxxxxxxxxxxxxxxxxxxxxxxxxxxxxxxxxx

Another example of horizontal spacing is the justified margin. As you read this book, you can see that the words of text line up exactly on the left and the right margins. Our trusty typesetter is putting imperceptible amounts of space between words, stretching out the line to produce the even right-hand margin. If your entries have a lot of text, the justified margin can look quite nice. If, on the other hand, your entries are brief, do not justify the text. Otherwise, you may get stuff that looks like this:

Education: University of North Carolina,   Chapel   Hill,
NC. B.A in History May 1994.   Curriculum also
included more than 33 hours in   pre-med
courses.

If you have your resume word-processed, make certain the operator knows the tricks of producing justified text. We've seen plenty of examples that look just as terrible as this one.

Punctuation

The only really effective punctuation to use for graphic emphasis is the bullet (•), the asterisk (*), the boxed bullet (■), or other tasteful graphic devices, known as dingbats (for example, • or °). Some people insist on using the hyphen (-), but we believe the bullet or asterisk does the job of emphasizing quite a bit better. If you decide to use punctuation marks as graphic devices, be careful: If you overdo it, your resume will resemble a used-car ad.

The bullet or asterisk is best used to highlight a series of events or blocks of information within a single entry. Be certain, however, that each accented event has several lines of text. Otherwise, you'll have too many accents next to each other and end up with the used-car ad once again. Here is an example using bullets to set off accomplishments in a given employment position. If they were not used, the entries would be so large that the resume reviewer might be tempted to skip over them.

Employment:	**Acme Widgets International,** Salt Lake City, UT Territory Sales Manager. Initially employed as sales representative in 1977. Due to record-setting sales generated during the first two years, I was promoted to Sales Manager.

- Recruited, hired, and trained a sales force of 15 members. Managed and motivated these salespersons through personal follow-up, weekly sales meetings, and encouragement.
- Developed a sales training manual for the Utah territory. Due to highly successful results, the manual was adopted for use by the company nationwide.
- Increased sales in territory by 80% in the first year, 150% in the second year, and 400% in the third year.

Graphic Mistakes

Let's look at some typical mistakes people make with graphic emphasis.

Misemphasizing Headings

The most common mistake is emphasizing a heading but fail-
ing to emphasize a lead within the heading. It makes little sense
to draw the reader's eye to the word *Education* unless you also
try to draw the reader's eye to the lead within that heading. The
following example of this mistake is comparable to writing a
book, printing *Chapter One* in large letters on the first page,
and then including the chapter name in small letters as follows:
the end of the universe.

EDUCATION: B.A. History, May 1990, Yale University, New
Haven, CT

Graphically, that is backward, and should appear as follows:

Education: **YALE UNIVERSITY,** New Haven, Connecticut.
B.A. History, May 1990.

Underlining Words Already
Emphasized by Spacing

Many words in your resume are already emphasized by spacing. For example, your centered name at the top of the resume
all by itself is emphasized by spacing. Also, your left-margin
headings are emphasized by their spacing and their standing
alone along the left margin. Do not emphasize them again by
underlining. Avoid this:

<u>JAMES SMITH</u>

Home Address: School Address:
101 Main Street   444 Hometown Road
Bethesda, MD 12345   Baltimore, MD 22222
(301) 333-3333   (410) 332-1111

<u>OBJECTIVE:</u>   xxxxxxxxxxxxxxxxxxxxxxxxxxxxxxxxxxxxxxxxxx

<u>EDUCATION:</u>   xxxxxxxxxxxxxxxxxxxxxxxxxxxxxxxxxxxxxxxxxx
xxxxxxxxxxxxxxxxxxxxxxxxxxxxxxxxxxxxxxx
xxxxxxxxxxxxxxxxxxxxxxxxxxxxxxxxxxxxxxxxxx

Underlining a Series of Leads on Succeeding Lines

Remember that the underlining technique, or any other graphic device, is supposed to draw the eye of the reader to focus on certain information. If you overdo it, the result is a mess. Take a look at this:

Activities: <u>President</u>, Phe Phi Pho Phum Fraternity
<u>Treasurer</u>, Phe Phi Pho Phum Fraternity
<u>Rush Chairman</u>, Phe Phi Pho Phum Fraternity
<u>Editor-in-Chief</u>, *The Commentator* student newspaper
<u>Student Council Representative</u>
<u>Chairman</u>, Intramural Committee

The reader's eye isn't drawn to that busyness. Indeed, the reader hopes to be able to avoid it. This example should avoid any underlining, bold type, or capitalization. Just let the list sit there unadorned. Ironically, the absence of graphic emphasis will draw the reader's eye to the list.

Other Graphic Quirks

Resume writers, all wanting to set things off and make things stand out, will employ a vast array of weird graphic devices. The all-time records, in our experience, have to go to the architect we mentioned earlier who designed his resume like a blueprint and to the student who wanted his resume printed on paper bearing the image of a shade tree. Once, when I was running my resume service in Charlottesville, a customer came in proudly touting the "new resume look" he had achieved. His visual disaster contained no fewer than sixteen different typing fonts. A real mess. But even less egregious quirks can detract substantially from an otherwise well-written resume.

Many resume writers load their resumes with all sorts of dashes (—), slashes (/), bullets (•), colons (:), asterisks (*), parentheses (()), multiple margins, and other bothersome distortions. The result is this:

Activities: Phe Phi Pho Phum Fraternity—President:
9/1/92–9/1/93.
Duties included: -presiding over weekly meetings;
: -supervising Rush activities;
-maintaining university relations;
: -coordinating social events.
Also responsible for: *appointing committee
chairmen;
: *adhering to $75,000 budget;
: *chairing the Executive Committee.

Even though we have used a facetious example, we have seen plenty of resumes that adopt the strangest techniques for graphic emphasis. Avoid the quirks. Instead, use the tasteful and effective graphic devices we've discussed in creating a document that will survive the thirty-second scan and get you where you want to be: the let's-take-a-look pile.

Formatting Summary

In this chapter we've focused on the all-important techniques of formatting. The way you lay out information on your resume will say a great deal about you. A well-organized format shows a thoughtful person. Your format can actually control the eye of the beholder during that crucial thirty-second scan. The format itself might indeed make the employment manager slow down and actually read your resume.

That first impression is vital. Remember the importance of clothes in sizing somebody up. The clothing on your resume will make that first, vital impression—not its content or its writing style, but its appearance, its clothing. But appearance is only partially determined by format. Suppose you write a terrific resume, have a dynamite writing style, and a format that would win an award for superlative graphic design. And suppose you printed that resume on a brown paper bag, cheap onionskin, or lime green paper with pink borders, or even just plain old photocopy paper. Another element of appearance enters the picture: production.

When you first meet someone, two basic senses are at work: sight and sound. But if you shake that person's hand, another sense comes into play: touch. Your resume will be seen but not heard. It will, however, be touched. The employment manager will pick it up. Thus, when you produce your resume, you must be concerned with two senses: sight and touch. To be properly dressed your resume must have the right look and the right feel.

CHAPTER 7

A Firm Handshake

Resume Production

PICTURE YOUR RESUME SITTING in a pile of other resumes. Imagine the employment manager just finished reviewing the resume right above yours in the pile. Yours is next. She picks it up, feels it, and quickly looks at it. In those first few seconds only two senses are at work: sight and touch. Does an impression begin to form in her mind? You bet it does, just as an impression of a person begins to form immediately upon that first introduction, that first hello, that first handshake.

Most of the resumes in that pile wear blue jeans. Does yours? Even if it's properly written, structured, and formatted, it still might wear blue jeans. It must be properly produced before it can effectively respond to and control those first two senses of sight and touch.

Three Production Decisions

When you produce your resume, you've got to make three decisions: how to produce it, how to reproduce it to get the number of copies you want, and what type and color of paper to use for your copies.

First Decision: How to Produce Your Resume

There are four ways you can produce your resume: typing, typesetting, word processing, and desktop publishing. Each has advantages and disadvantages.

Typing Your Resume.   If you plan to type your resume yourself, be careful. Be certain you have a top-notch typewriter, one that makes the image by striking a carbon (not a cloth) ribbon. Be sure it has a correcting feature enabling you to strike out any mistakes (don't use correction fluid to correct mistakes; no matter how hard you try, the mistakes will still show on your copies). Make sure your underline character produces truly straight underscoring rather than a series of jagged lines. Be prepared to forego any boldfaced emphasis on your resume, as it is extremely difficult to produce on an ordinary typewriter. And finally, be ready to retype the resume many times, because you're likely to end up with either too little or too much space at the bottom of the page.

In a word, don't type your resume. Prepare to enter the twentieth century and use modern word processing or desktop publishing technology, if only because these methods give you an electronic file that can be easily revised. If you don't know anything about word processing or desktop publishing, then let a pro do it.

Typesetting Your Resume.   Typesetting these days is done by computer technology but, as we will explain, is generally more awkward and old-fashioned than other forms of creating your resume via computer. A typesetting machine actually photographs images of letters in a variety of fonts to produce a sheet of type. That type is then pasted up and positioned to produce camera-ready copy. The type you see in some books is still typeset in this fashion. Typeset looks better than typewritten, but should you use it on your resume? Possibly yes, but probably no, especially if you have access to either word processing or desktop publishing technology.

The primary problems with typeset resumes are cost and inconvenience. Taking your resume to a typesetter or a resume service using typesetting can cost you on the order of seventy-five to one hundred fifty dollars for the typesetting and twenty-five or so copies. Once you've got your resume typeset, it can be very difficult and costly to get it revised.

Word Processing or Desktop Publishing Your Resume. These days, the only way to go is to use modern word processing, or its more powerful cousins, the desktop page layout programs, to produce your resume. Because people are becoming accustomed to receiving word-processed, rather than typewritten, correspondence, word-processed resumes in effect look just as personal as typewritten resumes. The word-processed resume also can look typeset, which therefore looks expensive. The word-processed resume can be easily and inexpensively revised, and it can be prepared and tailored for a specific prospective employer. With a word processor you can experiment with different formats, you can use bold type, you can produce your text with a right-justified margin, you can make revisions and correct mistakes, and you can store your resume for future revision.

If you word process your resume, be careful when you select a printer. Make certain the equipment produces a truly sharp image. Take a careful look at the underlining feature to be sure it produces a straight and not a jagged line. Never print out your resume on a dot matrix printer. At least it must be an impact printer striking a carbon ribbon. Preferably it should be a laser printer with a resolution of 300 dots per inch.

You may also want to produce your resume using a desktop formatting or page layout program, such as PageMaker, Ventura, or Quark XPress. Although most word processing programs now include the basic formatting features you'll need for your resume, the formatting programs can offer you a wider range of options and greater flexibility in producing the exact look you want. You can also load the text of your resume from a word processing file into a formatting program for final production.

Desktop publishing gives you another printing option as well, beyond the laser printer. If you wish, you can take your page layout file to a publishing service bureau to have it printed out so that the type is as sharp and black as typesetting—1270 dots per inch, for example, rather than the 300 dots per inch generated by most laser printers. Because this procedure is often done through a machine called a Linotronic, it is often referred to as having your type lino'd. Although the difference between laser print and lino is readily discernible to publishing professionals, it's rather subtle to most people, so that laser printing is quite acceptable. Lino or typeset quality may be a reasonable option for people circulating their resumes in the design and communications fields, but even here laser-printed resumes are the rule, because of their convenience. The cost of lino is reasonable—five to fifteen dollars a page, so that a two-page typeset-quality resume ready for photocopying will cost less than thirty dollars—yet the bother and repeated expense of going to a service bureau every time you need to revise your resume probably isn't justified by the subtle difference in type.

To summarize, we believe the word-processed or desktop published resume provides the best results. If you do type your resume, get it done by a professional. If you have your resume typeset, be sure you make the font and formatting decisions based on what you've learned in this book. If you take your resume to someone else for word processing or desktop publishing, the same caution applies. Be sure to specify not only font but also type size—or make it clear in advance that you will be reviewing the first draft and specifying any changes you want. Be sure you control the types of graphic emphasis employed. Resumes left solely to the discretion of a typesetter or even a desktop publishing designer can end up looking like used-car commercials, complete with balloons and dancing bears.

Word Processing It Yourself.   Many people these days know how to use word processing software programs such as WordPerfect, Microsoft Word, WordStar, MacWrite, and IBM Display Write. Unfortunately, many people do not know the full extent of the word processor's powers. They don't know how to set proper margins, select the proper fonts, produce bullets or other dingbats, right justify lines, produce indentations, and so on. Turned loose with a word processor, many people will produce some absolutely awful resumes (just ask the recruiters who have to review them).

Second Decision: How to Reproduce Your Resume

You've got a good, clean original of your resume. You've produced it by a good typewriter, a good typesetter, or a good word processor or page layout program. Now you've got to reproduce it. There are only three ways to reproduce the copies you need. You can have your resume printed, you can laser-print multiple copies from your word processing or page layout files, or you can have it photocopied.

If you take your original resume to a printer, be sure the printer has the right kind of paper (see the discussion of paper selection below). If that printer does not have the proper paper, find one that does. If you can't find one that stocks the right paper, find out where you can buy it, then take the necessary supply of paper with you to the printer. Before you order copies from the printer, be sure to ask for some samples. Make certain the printer can produce copies without the slightest extraneous dot or smudge.

Another way is to laser-print multiple copies of your resume rather than take the master laser originals to be printed on a press or photocopied. One problem with this option has to do with the health and welfare of your laser printer—it may be wiser and, in the long run, cheaper to take your master copy to a photocopy shop. Another problem is more compelling: although you can use a variety of papers in your laser printer, some laser printer manufacturers ask you not to use the type of paper we strongly recommend for your resume (100 percent rag paper). Recently, paper manufacturers have introduced 100 percent cotton paper specifically designed for laser printers.

The other way to reproduce your resume is to have it photocopied. Here you have to be extremely careful. First, be sure the copy center has the right kind of paper (as revealed below). Second, ask the copy center to run two copies of your resume before you commit to ordering fifty or one hundred. Why two? Because the drums of many photocopiers make two impressions. If the drum has a speck on it, it might not show up on just one copy but would show up on the next copy. Carefully check the two copies and make certain you find absolutely no specks or flecks on either copy. If you do, ask the copy center to get rid of the specks by cleaning either the screen or the drum. If they can't, find another copy center that can produce fleckless copies.

Third Decision: Kind and Color of Paper to Use

As to paper type there is only one pat answer. Insist on paper made of 100 percent cotton fiber. In the trade this is called rag content. Be sure you specify 100 percent rag. Why not 50 percent or 25 percent cotton? Because of feel. If you take a piece of 100 percent cotton paper and a piece of 25 percent cotton paper in your hands at the same time, you'll notice the 100 percent cotton paper feels richer, finer, and more professional.

Is feel important? Of course it is. When an employment manager picks up your resume, that's the first contact he has with you. He feels your resume even before he sees it. That's the first handshake. In an interview you would not offer the interviewer a limp, dead-fish handshake. Then why should your resume feel like a dead fish? It shouldn't. It should be a firm and confident handshake. Only 100 percent cotton paper can do the job.

What about color? There are only three acceptable colors: white, off-white or ivory, and gray. If you use off-white or ivory, be sure it is just a subtle tan. Don't go with any distinctly brown paper or any unusual tan color; we've seen some so-called off-white paper that resembles a grocery bag. It should be very subtle. The same is true with gray: it should be subtle, and not silver. Of course, it should go without saying that you'd never use any pastel colors or other weird shades, but we say it anyway, because we've heard about some strange paper requests for printing resumes (the most recent was a dark shade of blue).

What color is right for you? It really depends on your targeted audience. If you're pursuing a conservative profession like banking or the law, stick with white or maybe a very subtle off-white. If you're going into the business world, then any of the three colors is all right. If you're going into the entertainment or other artistic field, then you might decide to use gray or a slightly darker tan.

Does this whole color business make any difference? A recent study showed resume reviewers prefer off-white or ivory (probably because it's easier on the eyes when they're reviewing more than eighty resumes each night).

Matching Your Cover Letters

One consideration might help you with the paper decision: your cover letters. First of all, your resume paper should match your cover-letter paper. So when you order resumes, be sure to order additional blank paper if you're typing your cover letters yourself. And if you are typing your own cover letters, you should select white paper. Why? Because you can strike out errors in your letters more easily on white than you can on ivory or gray.

Professional Resume Services

You can check the yellow pages in most telephone books and find numerous resume services in most American cities. Before you commit to using a professional service, you should ask to see some sample resumes, inquire about the paper used, see whether the service will electronically store your resume for future revision, and ask for a firm cost estimate. Prices will range from nine dollars for a typed resume with no copies to several hundred dollars for professional writing services.

If you wish to retain a professional writer, definitely ask for references, and check out the references before committing to the service. Ask for a price range on the phone. If the service refuses to give you a price range, stay away from that service!

Watch out for self-proclaimed experts. At many colleges and universities, you'll find scads of professional resume writer notices on bulletin boards. We once worked with a professional editor from New York who had paid a professional eighty dollars for resume-writing services. The resume she received was a disaster. So be careful. Ask the resume writer for his or her resume, as well as for references, and check those references out!

Whether you use a professional service, hire a typist, or do it yourself, you should follow the instructions in this chapter on the techniques of resume production and reproduction. Some people might sniff at the notion that production makes a difference. But you've got to agree that the first contact the employment manager has with you is that moment when he touches your resume. He picks it up, feels it, and then begins to read it. Shake his hand, firmly and convincingly.

CHAPTER 8

Who Is
Justinius Regal?
Sample Resume Formats

THROUGHOUT THIS BOOK WE'VE provided samples of resumes. Although the anecdotes we've shared do involve real people (with totally changed circumstances to protect their privacy), all examples of resume entries represent fictitious people whose education, employment, activities, interests, and so on came only from our imaginations. We don't think there's a Bill's Bar and Grill in Chattanooga, Tennessee. And we certainly hope there is no Justinius Regal, whom you'll meet shortly.

Copying Resumes Is
Hazardous to Your Career

The resume samples in this book are fictitious, but perhaps they resemble your situation. Maybe, for example, you really did "earn a 3.1 GPA while working 20 hours per week during the academic year." We know you may be tempted to borrow those words when you write your own resume. The problem, of course, is that thousands of other readers of this scintillating bestseller might be similarly tempted. Your resume absolutely must be a highly personal and unique document. Do not follow any resume book and borrow the descriptions of positions similar to yours. Don't follow the headings of any other resume and try to plug your life into those headings. Your life won't fit somebody else's resume.

We once saw a very interesting phenomenon at the University of Virginia. All the education school resumes looked alike, with similar formats and headings. All the law school resumes looked alike as well. Same with the commerce school. Why? Students shared their resumes with underclassmen. Various placement offices had sample resumes on file. And, quite naturally, when a student or anybody else tackled the imposing task of constructing a resume, the temptation was overwhelming to borrow from another resume.

The same phenomenon probably occurs within other universities and within professional and business offices across the country. And what happens? We once reviewed the resume of a college senior. He had considerable experience in computers. He constructed his resume using a standard sample in the placement office of his university. That resume was a functional resume that had these headings: Creativity, Leadership, and Writing Ability. This student, like hundreds of others, adopted these headings and tried to squeeze his life into them. His life didn't fit. His resulting resume literally buried his substantial experience in computer programming and computer operations. We convinced him to discard the copied headings and to create his own: Computer Experience, Programming Experience, Computer Operations. This way he touted his very considerable credentials and ended up with a first-rate resume.

Use what you've learned in this book. Choose the kind of resume you want, devise the content and structure, create your own headings, entries, and leads, make your own decisions about the relevance of your dates, and develop your own strategy and graphic devices to hammer home your strongest attributes, your skills, your job objective, and your most impressive leads. But please don't copy the examples in this book!

Copying Formats Is Not So Hazardous

Formatting is a bit different. There probably is a finite number of formats that could be created to produce the results you want: a well-dressed resume with a firm, enthusiastic handshake. In fact, if you try to get too creative in the art of formatting, you just might end up with the blueprint or shade-tree resumes we joked about earlier. Or you might produce a used-car ad complete with balloons and dancing bears. So there's nothing wrong with borrowing formats. To that end we've put together some samples in the pages that follow. These represent suggestions only. Each one can be altered and tailored to fit your needs and strategies. Nothing is magic about these formats; they are not necessarily the best formats ever created. They are just some suggestions that follow our rules on neatness and proper graphic emphasis. Feel free then to construct your resume along the lines of the following formats.

Copying resumes can be so hazardous to your career that we've devised a special no-copying control system to discourage your copying the text in the following sample formats. We think we've made certain you will create your own headings, devise your own leads, place your dates in the proper place, and write your own entries to show that employment manager you have the right stuff. After all, who on earth could copy the life of Justinius Regal? Who on earth would want to?

Format 1: Plain and Simple, Left-Margin Headings

JUSTINIUS REGAL
100 LeDeaux Enclave
New Orleans, LA 44422
(101) 111-1111 (home)
(101) 345-6789 (auto)

Objective: To assume a position of major responsibility in the wine industry.

Education: Le Vin d'Institute Magnifique, Paris, France.
B.S. in Chablis and Brie, May 1993. Coursework included Proper Attire, Olfactory Sensing of Less Than Satisfactory Vintages, Glass Swirling, Baritone Voice Control, and the Art of Hiding an American Accent. GPA = 3.1 in Brie.

Awards: Received the Brow Award (recognizing unique aptitude for assuming a quizzical mien) and the Better Burgundy Accent on English Award (placed first in wine advertising competition sponsored by the American Wine Industry Advertising Bureau).

Fine Wine Maltese Manor, Tuscany Hills, California.
Experience: Initially employed in the Grape Crushing Department of this world-renowned winery known primarily for its use of ancient techniques. Instituted a quality and sanitation control system since adopted by most major wineries and currently known as Ped Agree. Due to immediate successful performance, advanced quickly to the Wine Tasting Department and was asked to return for an additional summer. Summers 1992, 1991.

Seminar Marketing Associates, Walnut, California.
Wine & Cheese Party Coordinator. Worked 50 hours per week during summer after freshman year in college setting up suburban wine and cheese parties to promote a variety of wine and cheese products. Selected the most appropriate locations, leased space, developed all promotions, and procured the obligatory disposable cups. Developed a unique system for rapidly producing and re-using wine bottle candleholders with intriguing drip designs. Series of parties that summer produced a 25% increase in wine and cheese sales. Summer 1990.

Activities: Founder & President, The Annie Green Springs Memorial Society. President, LeDeaux Chapter, Volvo Enthusiast Clubs of America. Treasurer, *New York Times* Weekly Readers Club.

Languages: Fluent in French. Well-developed English accent.

Travel: In addition to studying in France for 4 years, extensively toured the Continent on 8 different occasions. Visited the major vineyards in France, Italy, and Germany. Also condescended to make token appearances at Spanish and Portuguese wine-making facilities.

Interests: Collecting monogrammed tennis racket covers.

References: Excellent professional references will be provided upon request.

Format 2: Bold and Brassy, Left-Margin Headings

JUSTINIUS REGAL
100 LeDeaux Enclave
New Orleans, LA 44422
(101) 111-1111 (home)
(101) 345-6789 (auto)

Objective: To assume a position of major responsibility in the wine industry.

Education: **LE VIN D'INSTITUTE MAGNIFIQUE,** Paris, France.
B.S. in Chablis and Brie, May 1993. Coursework included Proper Attire, Olfactory Sensing of Less Than Satisfactory Vintages, Glass Swirling, Baritone Voice Control, and the Art of Hiding an American Accent. **GPA = 3.1 in Brie.**

Awards: Received the Brow Award (recognizing unique aptitude for assuming a quizzical mien) and the Better Burgundy Accent on English Award (placed first in wine advertising competition sponsored by the American Wine Industry Advertising Bureau).

Fine Wine **MALTESE MANOR,** Tuscany Hills, California.
Experience: Initially employed in the Grape Crushing Department of this world-renowned winery known primarily for its use of ancient techniques. Instituted a quality and sanitation control system since adopted by most major wineries and currently known as Ped Agree. Due to immediate successful performance, advanced quickly to the Wine Tasting Department and was asked to return for an additional summer. Summers 1992, 1991.

SEMINAR MARKETING ASSOCIATES, Walnut, California.
Wine & Cheese Party Coordinator. Worked 50 hours per week during summer after freshman year in college setting up suburban wine and cheese parties to promote a variety of wine and cheese products. Selected the most appropriate locations, leased space, developed all promotions, and procured the obligatory disposable cups. Developed a unique system for rapidly producing and re-using wine bottle candleholders with intriguing drip designs. Series of parties that summer produced a 25% increase in wine and cheese sales. Summer 1990.

Activities: **Founder & President,** The Annie Green Springs Memorial Society. **President,** LeDeaux Chapter, Volvo Enthusiast Clubs of America. **Treasurer,** *New York Times* Weekly Readers Club.

Languages: Fluent in French. Well-developed English accent.

Travel: In addition to studying in France for 4 years, extensively toured the Continent on 8 different occasions. Visited the major vineyards in France, Italy, and Germany. Also condescended to make token appearances at Spanish and Portuguese wine-making facilities.

Interests: Collecting monogrammed tennis racket covers.

References: Excellent professional references will be provided upon request.

Format 3: Centered and Bold Headings, Bold Leads

JUSTINIUS REGAL
100 LeDeaux Enclave
New Orleans, LA 44422
(101) 111-1111 (home)
(101) 345-6789 (auto)

CAREER OBJECTIVE

To assume a position of major responsibility in the wine industry.

EDUCATION

Le Vin d'Institute Magnifique, Paris, France. B.S. in Chablis and Brie, May 1993. Coursework included Proper Attire, Olfactory Sensing of Less Than Satisfactory Vintages, Glass Swirling, Baritone Voice Control, and the Art of Hiding an American Accent. GPA = 3.1 in Brie.

Awards: Received the Brow Award (recognizing unique aptitude for assuming a quizzical mien) and the Better Burgundy Accent on English Award (placed first in wine advertising competition sponsored by the American Wine Industry Advertising Bureau).

FINE WINE EXPERIENCE

Maltese Manor, Tuscany Hills, California. Initially employed in the Grape Crushing Department of this world-renowned winery known primarily for its use of ancient techniques. Instituted a quality and sanitation control system since adopted by most major wineries and currently known as Ped Agree. Due to immediate successful performance, advanced quickly to the Wine Tasting Department and was asked to return for an additional summer. Summers 1992, 1991.

Seminar Marketing Associates, Walnut, California. Wine & Cheese Party Coordinator. Worked 50 hours per week during summer after freshman year in college setting up suburban wine and cheese parties to promote a variety of wine and cheese products. Selected the most appropriate locations, leased space, developed all promotions, and procured the obligatory disposable cups. Developed a unique system for rapidly producing and reusing wine bottle candleholders with intriguing drip designs. Series of parties that summer produced a 25% increase in wine and cheese sales. Summer 1990.

ACTIVITIES

Founder & President, The Annie Green Springs Memorial Society. **President,** LeDeaux Chapter, Volvo Enthusiast Clubs of America. **Treasurer,** *New York Times* Weekly Readers Club.

FOREIGN TRAVEL

In addition to studying in France for 4 years, extensively toured the Continent on 8 different occasions. Visited the major vineyards in France, Italy, and Germany. Also condescended to make token appearances at Spanish and Portuguese wine-making facilities.

Excellent professional references will be provided upon request.

Format 4: Left-Margin Headings, Indented Entries

JUSTINIUS REGAL
100 LeDeaux Enclave
New Orleans, LA 44422
(101) 111-1111 (home)
(101) 345-6789 (auto)

Objective:

To assume a position of major responsibility in the wine industry.

Education:

Le Vin d'Institute Magnifique, Paris, France. B.S. in Chablis and Brie, May 1993. Coursework included Proper Attire, Olfactory Sensing of Less Than Satisfactory Vintages, Glass Swirling, Baritone Voice Control, and the Art of Hiding an American Accent. GPA = 3.1 in Brie.

Awards: Received the Brow Award (recognizing unique aptitude for assuming a quizzical mien) and the Better Burgundy Accent on English Award (placed first in wine advertising competition sponsored by the American Wine Industry Advertising Bureau).

Fine Wine Experience:

Maltese Manor, Tuscany Hills, California. Initially employed in the Grape Crushing Department of this world-renowned winery known primarily for its use of ancient techniques. Instituted a quality and sanitation control system since adopted by most major wineries and currently known as Ped Agree. Due to immediate successful performance, advanced quickly to the Wine Tasting Department and was asked to return for an additional summer. Summers 1992, 1991.

Seminar Marketing Associates, Walnut, California. Wine & Cheese Party Coordinator. Worked 50 hours per week during summer after freshman year in college setting up suburban wine and cheese parties to promote a variety of wine and cheese products. Selected the most appropriate locations, leased space, developed all promotions, and procured the obligatory disposable cups. Developed a unique system for rapidly producing and reusing wine bottle candleholders with intriguing drip designs. Series of parties that summer produced a 25% increase in wine and cheese sales. Summer 1990.

Activities:

Founder & President, The Annie Green Springs Memorial Society. **President,** LeDeaux Chapter, Volvo Enthusiast Clubs of America. **Treasurer,** *New York Times* Weekly Readers Club.

Foreign Travel:

In addition to studying in France for 4 years, extensively toured the Continent on 8 different occasions. Visited the major vineyards in France, Italy, and Germany. Also condescended to make token appearances at Spanish and Portuguese wine-making facilities.

Excellent professional references will be provided on request.

Format 5: Paragraph Format, Justified Text

JUSTINIUS REGAL
100 LeDeaux Enclave
New Orleans, LA 44422
(101) 111-1111 (home)
(101) 345-6789 (auto)

Objective: To assume a position of major responsibility in the wine industry.

Education: *Le Vin d'Institute Magnifique,* Paris, France. *B.S. in Chablis and Brie,* May 1993. Coursework included Proper Attire, Olfactory Sensing of Less Than Satisfactory Vintages, Glass Swirling, Baritone Voice Control, and the Art of Hiding an American Accent. GPA = 3.1 in Brie.

Awards: Received the Brow Award (recognizing unique aptitude for assuming a quizzical mien) and the Better Burgundy Accent on English Award (placed first in wine advertising competition sponsored by the American Wine Industry Advertising Bureau).

Fine Wine Experience: *Maltese Manor,* Tuscany Hills, California. Initially employed in the Grape Crushing Department of this world-renowned winery known primarily for its use of ancient techniques. Instituted a quality and sanitation control system since adopted by most major wineries and currently known as Ped Agree. Due to immediate successful performance, advanced quickly to the Wine Tasting Department and was asked to return for an additional summer. Summers 1992, 1991.

Seminar Marketing Associates, Walnut, California. Wine & Cheese Party Coordinator. Worked 50 hours per week during summer after freshman year in college setting up suburban wine and cheese parties to promote a variety of wine and cheese products. Selected the most appropriate locations, leased space, developed all promotions, and procured the obligatory disposable cups. Developed a unique system for rapidly producing and reusing wine bottle candleholders with intriguing drip designs. Series of parties that summer produced a 25% increase in wine and cheese sales. Summer 1990.

Activities: *Founder & President,* The Annie Green Springs Memorial Society. *President,* LeDeaux Chapter, Volvo Enthusiast Clubs of America. *Treasurer, New York Times* Weekly Readers Club.

Languages: Fluent in French. Well-developed English accent.

Foreign Travel: In addition to studying in France for 4 years, extensively toured the Continent on 8 different occasions. Visited the major vineyards in France, Italy, and Germany. Also condescended to make token appearances at Spanish and Portuguese wine-making facilities.

Interests: Collecting monogrammed tennis racket covers.

References: Excellent professional references will be provided upon request.

Format 6: Left-Margin Headings, Bullets

JUSTINIUS REGAL
100 LeDeaux Enclave
New Orleans, LA 44422
(101) 111-1111 (home)
(101) 345-6789 (auto)

Objective: To assume a position of major responsibility in the wine industry.

Education: **LE VIN D'INSTITUTE MAGNIFIQUE,** Paris, France.
B.S. in Chablis and Brie, May 1993. Coursework included Proper Attire, Olfactory Sensing of Less Than Satisfactory Vintages, Glass Swirling, Baritone Voice Control, and the Art of Hiding an American Accent. GPA = 3.1 in Brie.

Awards: Received the Brow Award (recognizing unique aptitude for assuming a quizzical mien) and the Better Burgundy Accent on English Award (placed first in wine advertising competition sponsored by the American Wine Industry Advertising Bureau).

Fine Wine **MALTESE MANOR,** Tuscany Hills, CA, Summers 1991, 1992.
Experience: • Initially employed in the Grape Crushing Department of this world-renowned winery known primarily for its use of ancient techniques.
• Instituted a quality and sanitation control system since adopted by most major wineries and currently known as Ped Agree. Due to immediate successful performance, advanced quickly to the Wine Tasting Department and was asked to return for an additional summer.

SEMINAR MARKETING ASSOCIATES, Walnut, CA, Summer 1990.
Wine & Cheese Party Coordinator.
• Worked 50 hours per week during summer after freshman year in college setting up suburban wine and cheese parties to promote a variety of wine and cheese products. Selected the most appropriate locations, leased space, developed all promotions, and procured the obligatory disposable cups.
• Developed a unique system for rapidly producing and reusing wine bottle candleholders with intriguing drip designs.
• Series of parties that summer produced a 25% increase in wine and cheese sales.

Activities: *Founder & President,* The Annie Green Springs Memorial Society. *President,* LeDeaux Chapter, Volvo Enthusiast Club. *Treasurer, New York Times* Weekly Readers Club.

Languages: Fluent in French. Well-developed English accent.

Travel: In addition to studying in France for 4 years, extensively toured the Continent on 8 different occasions. Visited the major vineyards in France, Italy, and Germany. Also condescended to make token appearances at Spanish and Portuguese wine-making facilities.

References: Excellent professional references will be provided upon request.

Format 7: Dates Emphasized, Left-Margin Headings, Left-Margin Caption

JUSTINIUS REGAL
100 LeDeaux Enclave
New Orleans, LA 44422
(101) 111-1111 (home)
(101) 345-6789 (auto)

Objective: To assume a position of major responsibility in the wine industry.

Education: **Le Vin d'Institute Magnifique,** Paris, France.
B.S. in Chablis and Brie, May 1993. Coursework included Proper Attire, Olfactory Sensing of Less Than Satisfactory Vintages, Glass Swirling, Baritone Voice Control, and the Art of Hiding an American Accent. GPA = 3.1 in Brie.

Awards: Received the Brow Award (recognizing unique aptitude for assuming a quizzical mien) and the Better Burgundy Accent on English Award (placed first in wine advertising competition sponsored by the American Wine Industry Advertising Bureau).

Fine Wine Experience:
Maltese Manor, Tuscany Hills, California, Summers 1991, 1992. Initially employed in the Grape Crushing Department of this world-renowned winery known primarily for its use of ancient techniques. Instituted a quality and sanitation control system since adopted by most major wineries and currently known as Ped Agree. Due to immediate successful performance, advanced quickly to the Wine Tasting Department and was asked to return for an additional summer.

Seminar Marketing Associates, Walnut, California, Summers 1990. *Wine & Cheese Party Coordinator.* Worked 50 hours per week during summer after freshman year in college setting up suburban wine and cheese parties to promote a variety of wine and cheese products. Selected the most appropriate locations, leased space, developed all promotions, and procured the obligatory disposable cups. Developed a unique system for rapidly producing and re-using wine bottle candleholders with intriguing drip designs. Series of parties that summer produced a 25% increase in wine and cheese sales.

Activities: **Founder & President,** The Annie Green Springs Memorial Society.
President, LeDeaux Chapter, Volvo Enthusiast Clubs of America.
Treasurer, *New York Times* Weekly Readers Club.

Languages: Fluent in French. Well-developed English accent.

Travel: In addition to studying in France for 4 years, extensively toured the Continent on 8 different occasions. Visited the major vineyards in France, Italy, and Germany. Also condescended to make token appearances at Spanish and Portuguese wine-making facilities.

Interests: Collecting monogrammed tennis racket covers.

References: Excellent professional references will be provided upon request.

Format 8: Double-Indented Paragraphs, Justified Text

JUSTINIUS REGAL
100 LeDeaux Enclave
New Orleans, LA 44422
(101) 111-1111 (home)
(101) 345-6789 (auto)

Objective
To assume a position of major responsibility in the wine industry.

Education
Le Vin d'Institute Magnifique, Paris, France.
B.S. in Chablis and Brie, May 1993. Coursework included Proper Attire, Olfactory Sensing of Less Than Satisfactory Vintages, Glass Swirling, Baritone Voice Control, and the Art of Hiding an American Accent. GPA = 3.1 in Brie. **Awards:** Received the Brow Award (recognizing unique aptitude for assuming a quizzical mien) and the Better Burgundy Accent on English Award (placed first in wine advertising competition sponsored by the American Wine Industry Advertising Bureau).

Fine Wine Experience
Maltese Manor, Tuscany Hills, California.
Initially employed in the Grape Crushing Department of this world-renowned winery known primarily for its use of ancient techniques. Instituted a quality and sanitation control system since adopted by most major wineries and currently known as Ped Agree. Due to immediate successful performance, advanced quickly to the Wine Tasting Department and was asked to return for an additional summer. Summers 1992, 1991.

Seminar Marketing Associates, Walnut, California.
Wine & Cheese Party Coordinator. Worked 50 hours per week during summer after freshman year in college setting up suburban wine and cheese parties to promote a variety of wine and cheese products. Selected the most appropriate locations, leased space, developed all promotions, and procured the obligatory disposable cups. Developed a unique system for rapidly producing and reusing wine bottle candleholders with intriguing drip designs. Series of parties that summer produced a 25% increase in wine and cheese sales. Summer 1990.

Activities
Founder & President, The Annie Green Springs Memorial Society. *President,* LeDeaux Chapter, Volvo Enthusiast Clubs of America. *Treasurer, New York Times* Weekly Readers Club.

Foreign Travel
In addition to studying in France for 4 years, extensively toured the Continent on 8 different occasions. Visited the major vineyards in France, Italy, and Germany. Also condescended to make token appearances at Spanish and Portuguese wine-making facilities.

Excellent professional references will be provided upon request.

CHAPTER 9

How to Dig for Paydirt

Prospecting

IT'S ALMOST TIME TO take the advertising piece you've been creating and search for opportunities to get an interview. First, however, you need to harken back to the end of Chapter 2 and recall your self-quiz concerning money, location, and job. Unless your job-search goal was already crystal clear to you then, it's a good idea to go back and clarify it now in light of all you've learned while putting together your resume. Then you'll be in the best position to follow the steps in this chapter to research your market and get interviews.

Surveying Your Market

In order to sell a product, companies and corporations spend millions of dollars on market analysis and research to find out what appeals to buyers. They find out what kind of buyer will be interested in a particular product and what product modifications might appeal to a larger or more desirable market. Market research can even tell the company roughly what a consumer will pay for a product or service. Companies that do effective market research generally are successful when they introduce their products. Others pay little or no attention to research, and consequently are not very successful.

Your job search must also be based on accurate, timely information about your market. If you enter the marketplace in search of meaningful employment without an adequate idea of what your market is, you are committed to failure.

Throughout this book we've talked mostly about defining the qualities you have that will appeal to the buyer—the employing company, nonprofit organization, or government agency. Now you must also search the marketplace of organizations to determine what they have for you, so that you can find the best fit between your attributes and needs and a company's attributes and needs. Fortunately for you, the market information you need for your job search is readily available for the taking. Your only investment will be the time necessary to gather it. Those of you who are just now planning a career or job change will probably be able to take most of the following steps in methodical fashion; if you're already in the midst of a change and you need to find work right away, you can adapt the steps to your needs, using them as a guide and following those that seem most appropriate for you.

Where to Start: The Library

For those of you who have time to prepare, the best places to gather information are the reference sections of your local college or university library, or the library of your local college's placement or career planning office. These libraries tend to be up to date and carry a wide selection of reference books to aid in your research. Such a wide variety of information is available that you could easily be overcome by the sheer volume of it all.

The advantage of a good placement or career planning office library, which is open to students and alumni, is that job-search sources are all accessible in one location, and someone with experience in this field may be available to give you assistance.

In any case, it will help to know what you're looking for. This will minimize the amount of time you have to spend poring over volume after volume on the same subject. Because you may need to make several visits, it's good to have a goal for each visit. An overall goal will be to compile a listing of potential employers that can be targeted.

What You Want to Find: Begin a Target List

Try to identify organizations engaged in your field of work, in the geographic area where you live. If you're seriously thinking of relocating, your first step is to check out the area where you want to settle, or where a job might be available. If you're considering a major career change, you may also need to get some ideas on various career fields you're qualified to enter. You can then develop lists of names and addresses of companies and corporations in order to begin sending out broadcast letters to get some actual interviews.

Get to Know Your Profession

To improve your vocabulary in the language of your profession, it is important to begin reading periodicals and trade journals. This will also help to expand your knowledge of specific organizations before an interview and might help in developing more leads for your campaign. You should also identify associations and groups that are in business to enhance or promote the overall image and professionalism of members and organizations in your field. You can contact them to join or merely to receive copies of their periodic publications.

Learn About the Companies or Organizations. For almost all of you who are over thirty, and any others already established in a business, trade, or profession, you have to learn about the companies or organizations you will be approaching. Not only will this research help you later when you begin to prospect for vacancies, but it becomes extremely significant when you go for an interview. You cannot afford to interview for an important position with a company unless you have some background information about that organization. It is critical, for example, to know whether a company is making money or losing money. What has their stock been doing for the past several months or for the past year? Has the company been successful in winning contracts, or has it lost some? Is the company the subject of a hostile takeover or a future merger? Have there been some recent management changes? Is there a record of hiring executives from outside the company, or do they promote from within? All of this information is readily available and can be located during an afternoon or two at the library.

How Much Are You Worth?   Finally, you may need to get more information concerning what you're worth to a potential employer. The cardinal rule to keep in mind is that you are only worth what your skills are worth in a specific marketplace. A switchboard operator in Detroit makes somewhere in the neighborhood of $200 a week. The same person doing the same job in Corpus Christi makes about $175 a week. The salary you can command doesn't have anything to do with what you want or what you're currently being paid, only with the value of your services in a specific job situation.

For many of you, information on your worth will start coming in piecemeal in the employment ads of your metropolitan newspaper. If you also want an overview for a specific field in a given geographic area, with the help of the librarian you will find volumes of information concerning salary and benefit packages. There are books written on specific career fields, articles on compensation packages, and stories about geographic differences. Some publications have even created charts to show how to rate specific metropolitan areas. As discussed earlier, your choice of location is going to have a lot to do with the median salary you can expect in your field.

How to Find Information at the Library

When you arrive at the library, walk around and familiarize yourself with the layout of the reference section, and then head

for the locator card or computer file. Review the file on directories first to see what is generally available, and write down
items that appear to offer the kinds of information you need.
You will discover that there are hundreds of directories, listing
every imaginable bit of information you would ever want. Be
careful that those you select to review are current. There's no
point in sending a letter to the CEO of a corporation when he
has been dead and buried for ten years.

One of the first directories to review will be the *Directory
of Directories*, published by Gale Research Co., Detroit, Michigan. This book will help you move quickly through the maze
and focus on what you need for your job search. Another good
starting source is the *Directory of Information Services*, published by Detroit Information Enterprises. This reference peri-
odical covers business and industrial directories, scientific and
professional rosters, and other lists and guides of all kinds.

Some other books you should review are *Ward's Directory
of the Largest U.S. Corporations*, *Ward's Directory of Private
U.S. Corporations*, and *Fortune's Directory of U.S. Corporations*.
These books will give you names and addresses of companies
and corporate officers by geographic location and industry. To
locate information on specific industries you should look at
books like *Emerson's Directory of Leading U.S. Accounting
Firms* and the *National League of Cities Directory of Local
Chief Executives, Elected and Administrative Officials*. Also
look in directories of companies doing business in various states
published by state economic development offices, directories
of companies doing business in foreign countries, state banking association directories, and others. A particularly good source
to find companies by geographic area or industry is *Duns Marketing Service Million Dollar Directories*.

Also, a must-read is *The National Job Bank* series, published by Bob Adams, Inc., Boston, Massachusetts. This series
has a job bank book for virtually every major city in the United
States. Each book provides the names, addresses, and telephone
numbers of hundreds of companies by state, along with the
names of the employment or personnel managers. You will also
find listed *A Directory of Employment Resources Offered by*

Associations and Other Organizations, which will provide you with even more information on helpful sources.

Don't forget to review *Rand McNally's Commercial Atlas* for statistical data including population, income, and growth patterns down to city and county level. You will also find listings of major companies doing business in the areas and the economic outlook for the future.

If you need to research specific companies, you should review *Where to Find Business Information*, published by John Wiley & Sons, New York, which will help keep you headed in the right direction. To locate current articles concerning specific industries or companies, spend some time browsing through the *Business Periodicals Index* published annually by the H. W. Wilson Company. This will be your guide to articles in various publications on companies, people, industries, compensation, and issues. This source will also give you needed current information to help you prepare for interviews. To check out a specific company, take a look at *Standard and Poor's Corporation Records* for background, earnings, officers, number of employees, and contact information. Also, Moody's Investors Service publishes *Municipal and Government Manuals* as well as manuals on banking and finance, industrials, transportation, and public utilities. For the insurance industry, be sure to look at *Best's Guide*.

For salary information there is as much data available as there is on other subjects. The *Business Periodicals Index* is a good place to start to find out what has been written in the form of news and information stories. But you should also review John Wright's book, *The American Almanac of Jobs and Salaries*. For college grads, the College Placement Council's *Annual Salary Survey for College Graduates* will help to add to your information database. Review of this data will help you assess your value based upon your skills and the median incomes for various career fields.

Ads as Research Materials

The final subject for your research is the employment ad itself. Read every employment advertisement you can find for your field. Make notes on the qualifications listed in each ad. Note commonly used terms for specific qualifications, see if they apply to your own background, and, if they do, use these terms in your resume as functional subheadings or within the text of your entries.

As your research continues, be alert for leads on potential job vacancies. Pay particular attention to the trade journals for job advertisements. Also, check for articles written by executives in your field on subjects of interest to you. Make notes for future use. Watch for companies that win contracts to provide goods or services and that might be hiring someone with your skills. Look for management changes that might indicate a major shakeup in a company in the near future. All of these are leads for jobs and should be followed up with a letter (and a copy of your resume) offering your services based upon the specific reason you saw a potential opportunity. We'll discuss more on transmittal letters later.

A final source that can be a real asset is the *National Business Employment Weekly* (NBEW), published by the *Wall Street Journal*. This publication comes out every Sunday and contains a compilation of the employment ads from all the regional editions of the *Wall Street Journal* during the past week. It is especially helpful to job seekers with professional qualifications in various business-related fields. More importantly, the *NBEW* carries a number of stories each week written by employment executives with tips on the job search that can be particularly helpful in adjusting your marketing plan.

In many ways your research and job-search efforts will coincide. While seeking information you are obviously going to come across opportunities to get your resume into the hands of some executive who is seeking to fill a vacancy. You should always be alert for information that could help you land an interview.

No Rest for the Weary

Research is an ongoing process that will last throughout the job search. Initially you may have a steep learning curve as you collect information to get you started, such as reading this book.

Later, as you begin to land interviews, you will find it necessary to focus your research to check out potential employers, compensation, and benefits. Don't think you can go in blind. That can be a sure path to poor performance in the interview and to mediocrity in the kind of position vacancies you locate. The competition is stiff, and the best-prepared candidate is going to make the best impression. Remember, the job search is a full-time job in itself and demands your full time and attention. You are not going to be satisfied with just finding a job, so you have to invest the time and effort necessary to accomplish your goal of finding your new career.

Essentials of Prospecting

Everyone involved with sales is familiar with prospecting, which is the activity that finds someone to talk to. Most sales people know exactly how many people they need to contact to obtain an appointment, and how many people they need to see in person to make a sale. No one gets an appointment every time they try, or closes the sale every time they make a presentation. So the basic three-part rule for professional sales people is, you must talk to enough people, they have to be the right kind of people, and you have to tell them your story. All three of the actions must happen to ensure success. They are the keys to success in sales. To put it another way, now that you've created your ad and defined the core of your self-presentation, you must make sure that presentation gets to where it will do you some good.

Drumming Up Interviews

You have to get interviews to find a job, so let's concentrate on obtaining an interview. Understand that you are going to have to follow up on a lot of leads in order to get each interview. You probably won't be successful every time you try. You need to use all of the sources you can develop and rely on no single source (such as the newspaper) to find leads. Keep the three-part rule in mind throughout the job search and apply it every day. Unfortunately, you won't know how many people (leads) you have to contact in order to get an interview, so you have to go after significant numbers to increase your chances.

In drumming up interviews, you've got to focus on a central fact of life, a rule of nature, one of the great truths in the entire universe, the one guarantee I absolutely can make: There are only three ways you can let people know you want a job— you can call them on the phone, you can talk to them in person, or you can send them a letter. There are no other ways. Forget about hiring a skywriter, forget the blimp idea, forget the idea of plastering your name and qualifications on the backs of matchbooks. To search for employment, therefore, you have got to make telephone calls, make personal visits, and send out letters. Nothing else works, believe me.

Drumming Up Leads

Here are ways to uncover leads so that you can make telephone calls, make personal visits, and send out letters.

The Newspaper

The Sunday newspaper from the major metropolitan area where you'll be working will be your major source of leads. Unfortunately, it is also the major source for scads of other job seekers. Although you will find some great opportunities, the competition will be stiff. A good-sized display ad in a major paper could produce as many as 1,000 responses for the position. As discussed in an earlier chapter, not more than 10 percent of the respondents, and maybe as few as 1 percent, will get interviews. But you have as good a chance as everyone else in being called, so don't neglect this source.

Some job-search experts like to spout statistics about how few jobs are procured by responding to classified ads. They will tout instead the hidden job market. We have a different opinion.

First, if the job market is hidden, then, by definition, you can't find it. Second, the employers are not taking out expensive classified ads just for fun. They are seeking real people to fill real positions who will receive very real money for their services. Third, your job campaign will rely on all possible sources; to neglect the classifieds simply because somebody once found a job by bumping into someone in a laundromat would be ludicrous.

National Publications

National publications such as trade journals and the *NBEW* offer lots of advertisements for specifically qualified people and are a great source if you are willing to move to accept employment. The *NBEW* generally carries advertisements for positions above the $35,000 per year bracket. Again, these publications enjoy a wide readership, so there will be many people responding to the same ads.

A good long-term strategy is to study and respond to articles written by or about people in your field. Write to authors and praise the quality of their articles, or write to the subject of an article and respond constructively to what he or she is doing. People love praise. It makes them feel you are an excellent judge of character. (If you write to tell us how much you enjoy this book, we'll be convinced that you, indeed, are brilliant.) Tell the writer or the subject of the article about your situation and your job search. Send your resume and ask for advice on your marketing plan. That often gets your resume into the hands of a corporate executive (the article's author or subject). One friend of ours noted an article about the goals of a new city manager in the local paper. He responded to the article by writing to the manager directly and congratulating him on his plans for his term in office. He also explained that he had recently left the armed services and thought he could bring much in the way of training and experience to the manager's administration. Significantly, he stressed that he shared the views of the city manager. The letter was referred to the city personnel department, which wrote back and requested a resume for an upcoming position vacancy.

The Hidden Job Market

As we mentioned, many outplacement specialists refer to the so-called hidden job market as the best source of job vacancy leads. We can't imagine a manager or a company that would not advertise for a person to fill a vacant position. If it is a valid vacancy, the company can't afford to lose money by leaving the position open until some hidden candidate shows up. There are cases, however, where a manager knows a position will be vacant because of a future firing or promotion and cannot advertise yet. Further, the company may be anticipating a staff increase because of an upcoming contract award or projected branch opening. In those cases, you could be given first consideration if your resume is already on hand. To get your resume into the hands of managers who know they'll have an opening to fill, use a technique called networking. First, call or write everyone you know who is working in your field or industry. Be sure to include any associates with whom you've worked before. Ask them to float your resume through their company. Don't feel you're imposing on these people because you may be doing them a favor: many companies pay a bounty to employees for referring a qualified candidate who gets hired. (It's a lot cheaper to pay a bonus to an employee than to pay a large agency fee.)

Next, if you're a specialist or expert in any particular work involving a specific product, such as a given software program, computer hardware, or any type of machinery or equipment, consider writing to the manufacturer and including your resume. Explain that you've been working with their product for years and know almost as much about it as they do. Tell them how they can benefit from your services in manufacturing, development, customer service, maintenance, or sales. (Note: Most technical companies do not hire sales people to sell their product. They hire technicians and teach them how to sell.)

Don't forget companies that appealed to you during your research. If a company looks good to you because it has great benefits, close proximity to your choice of locations, or some other attraction, don't wait for a position vacancy to appear. Write to the company and tell them what attracted you. A well-stated reason could be an indicator of future loyalty to that company.

Finally, in general, take an active, or as they say, proactive, role toward any company you know is a natural for you. If there is an obvious connection between you and a prospective employing company, don't hesitate to write to that company, enclosing your resume, and let them know why you belong on their team. For example, an editor we know was well versed in a particular psychological theory, was well aware that the latest book on that theory had been published without the editing it needed, and was in need of a job. One day he put all this together, photocopied two pages out of the middle of the book, wrote in his suggested editorial changes, and mailed it, with cover letter and resume, to the author. Within a week he was hired as publications director of the large psychological clinic headed by that author.

Transmittal Letters

The cover letter or letter of transmittal can be your number one prospecting tool because it gives you a way to put your thoughts into the mind of a prospective employer. Be careful of the term *cover letter*, for it can imply a generic type of letter that is preprinted and used for every opportunity you pursue. All you do is date it and sign it. Further, most cover letters look pretty much the same to human resources types, and, if noticed at all, they only get a cursory glance. On the other hand, a letter of transmittal is used to transmit your resume for a specific purpose. It is individually drafted and typed, and uses original and unique wording that directly relates to the position or situation. It avoids old worn-out phrases like the plague. It's not easy to create a new letter every time you go after a vacancy, but in order to find meaningful employment, you are going to have to work a little bit harder.

If you've written, formatted, produced, and reproduced a wonderful resume, then you should pay as much care and attention to the cover letter that carries your resume to an employer.

After all, it really makes no sense to send a well-dressed resume to its destination in an old, banged-up jalopy. No, your resume should arrive in a limousine, with a transmittal letter that conveys the same professional traits you've touted in your resume.

Your letters to employers should use effective selling techniques to attain the goal of getting an interview. There are four major steps that must occur in order to sell a product: attention, interest, desire, and action, or AIDA. Simply explained and applied to your marketing plan, it works out like this:

1. A You have to get the *attention* of potential employers. The best way to do that is to put a well-prepared resume in their hands.

2. I *Interest* must be created by showing the employer you are qualified and have something to offer the company in the way of training or experience.

3. D The employer must have the *desire* to talk to you because your qualifications are more closely aligned with their needs than those of other candidates.

4. A The employer must be encouraged to take the *action* you want. In this case the action is to call you for an interview.

The letter of transmittal can help you accomplish the four steps.

The Three Paragraph Rule

The best transmittal letters are short and to the point. The employer doesn't have time to read a dissertation. Instead, honor the thirty-second rule and realize that regardless of what you say the employer is going to scan your letter, then put it in either the reject pile or the let's-take-a-look pile.

Rarely use more than three paragraphs to write your transmittal letter. The first paragraph should state who you are and what you want. The second paragraph should stress your strongest points and relate them directly to the position you seek.

The third paragraph should be essentially a close requesting definite action on the part of the reader. Let's look at each paragraph individually.

Paragraph 1: Who You Are and What You Want. In the first paragraph, introduce yourself and let the employer know why you're writing. Don't start out with, "My name is Justinius Regal. How are you this fine morning? I'd like a job with major responsibility in the wine industry." We've seen some start just like that. Instead, introduce yourself by directing the employer's attention to your current status. For example, "I am a graduating senior from the World University interested in launching my career in public relations with Consolidated Widgets." Or, "I am a senior vice president with Acme Manufacturing interested in exploring possible affiliation with Consolidated Tire."

Another effective point to stress in the first paragraph is your interest in the geographic location of the prospective employer. For example, "Though I have thoroughly enjoyed my education in the South, I have always planned to return to Peoria, where I have family and friends." Alternatively, you might include in the first paragraph some explanation of why you seek a new position. For example, "Although I have profited, both professionally and financially, during my seven years with Acme, I believe the time has come for a professional change."

The possibilities in the first paragraph are almost limitless. Later we'll discuss how you should vary the first paragraph depending on whether you're responding to a classified ad, following up on a personal lead, or sending out a mass mailing. The rule to remember is to keep it short and to the point.

Paragraph 2: How You Can Benefit the Employer. In the second paragraph you should sell yourself. Your perspective, however, should be the reader's. What can you offer the employer? How can your experience benefit the employer? What's in it for the employer (not what's in it for you)?

Most cover letters will begin the second paragraph with this terribly tortured and overused expression, "Enclosed you will find a copy of my resume," as if the employer has to look for it or doesn't expect you to include a resume. We've seen even stuffier beginnings: "Enclosed herewith please find a copy of my resume." Avoid these cliches.

Instead, direct the employer's attention to your strongest points and relate them to the needs of her organization. For example:

> As you can see on my enclosed resume, I have had a wealth of practical experience in public relations. My summer public relations jobs with Ernest and Jacoby gave me the chance to prepare from scratch no fewer than 24 separate press releases and proposed copy for 12 brochures. Certainly this experience, coupled with my Dean's List performance at World University, can benefit Acme substantially in its continuing efforts to maintain and improve its position in the widget industry.

In paragraph 2 you should remember to use the techniques we discussed in Chapter 5. Use action verbs and numbers, and toot your horn. Show how you can help the company.

Here are some real-life examples. A young lawyer wanted to relocate from the Northeast to the Sun Belt. He had held a position for five years and had amassed considerable writing experience. Here's his middle paragraph:

> During the past five years I've prepared more than 75 trial briefs, 42 appellate briefs to the state intermediate appellate court, 17 appellate briefs to the state supreme court, and 74 briefs to the United States Court of Appeals for the Second Circuit. Subject matter in these cases has ranged from antitrust to complex federal tax matters, precisely the types of cases you confront in your practice. After you review my enclosed resume, I think you'll agree I possess the exact credentials you seek in your new associates.

Another good trick in the second paragraph is to point out how easy it would be for the employer to hire you. Most employers, especially in smaller organizations, don't like to hire new people. New people require a lot of time and money to assimilate and to train. They represent quite a risk if they don't work out. Here's what one successful job seeker wrote:

My experience is so substantial that I represent a risk-free addition to your staff. Little, if any, start-up time will be required before I am producing for you more than enough income to pay my salary several times over.

In the second paragraph you have just a few sentences to draw the employer's attention to your strongest points. You want to paint a vivid picture of the major benefits you can bring to the employer's organization.

Paragraph 3: The Call for Action.   Here's where most cover letters fail terribly. They end with this:

Thank you for your time and consideration. I hope to hear from you soon.

Hear what? That the employer doesn't want you? That the employer received your letter and will keep it on file? That she wishes you luck in the future? No, don't end that way. Tell the employer what you want her to do. Like any good salesperson, you have to close and close hard. Several possibilities exist.

If you're writing to a local employer, then your third paragraph should definitely ask for an interview right away. We've seen some very effective local cover letters close by asking, "When may we get together for a personal interview?" Not "may we," "*when* may we." If you're writing to an out-of-town employer and plan to be in that employer's area, then you should definitely say so. For example:

I plan to visit Peoria during the week of November 7–14 and will welcome the chance to meet you personally. Please let me hear from you right away.

Notice: Not "*would* welcome the chance," but "*will* welcome the chance." Quite simply, the third paragraph must be a call for action. Tell the employer exactly what you want her to do.

Some Dos and Don'ts

Include all possible telephone numbers in your return address, even if the same information appears in your resume. Make it easy for the employer to respond right away.

If you're currently employed, don't use your current employer's letterhead. The message you convey says you use company time and supplies to pursue your own ends.

Do not preach to the employer. This is a common mistake and turns the employer right off. For example, never begin a letter like this:

> In today's highly competitive business world companies must be extremely careful to control the quality of their products and services.

The employer knows that and doesn't want to hear it from some *applicant*.

Ending Your Letter

Do not end your letter stuffily, like this: "Thank you for your time and consideration of this matter. Anticipating your reply, I am, Sincerely yours, Justinius Regal." Instead, end crisply, like the following: "Thank you for your time. Sincerely yours, Justinius Regal."

When you sign your name, make your signature bold and assertive. Don't scratch in a tiny little signature the employer can hardly read. And use a fountain pen or one of those modern roller pens to sign your letters. Do not use a ballpoint. Dark blue or black ink is preferred.

Three Types of Transmittal Letters

You'll use a transmittal letter in three situations, responding to a classified ad, responding to a personal lead, and sending out a mass mailing.

Response to a Classified Ad.   Let's take a look at an employment advertisement and then develop a letter to go after the position. Employment advertisements have four major bits of information. First, they describe the company to get you excited and interested in joining their team. Second, they describe the position in glowing terms to make you want the job. Third, they list the qualifications for the position. And fourth, they provide response information.

Writing an advertisement is difficult. The author has to fit all four bits of information into a small space. If the ad doesn't describe the company or the position in the right terms, no one will apply. If it doesn't list the qualifications correctly, the wrong people might apply. If the response information is not drafted properly, the company might get deluged with phone calls it can't effectively handle, and the department will get bogged down.

When the replies come in, guess who reads the responses? You got it: the recruiter who wrote the ad. Wouldn't it be interesting if the recruiter read her own words when she received your letter and resume? Here is an example:

HIGH SPEED YO-YO OPERATOR

The XYZ Nut Fastener Company, a leader in the industry, has an immediate need for a high speed yo-yo operator in the Widget department. XYZ offers excellent benefits including profit sharing, paid vacation, medical, and 401K. To be considered, qualified candidates should be

- suave
- debonair
- devil-may-care

Experience should include five years in the field and management/supervisory experience. Candidates should possess BA/BS in Industrial Management.

Send resume with salary requirements to:
Employment Manager
XYZ Nut Fastener Company
P.O. Box 5555
Podunk, IL 66606

You have reviewed the ad and feel this is the job for you. To respond, you need to create a letter that will appeal to the recruiter who will do the initial screening, probably the person who drafted the ad. There are several important strategies to consider.

1. In the first paragraph include the position, as well as the name of the publication and the date that the ad appeared. The company may be running several ads for various positions in several different papers.

2. Address the letter to a specific person. If no name appears, call the company, tell them you are interested in the position, and ask to whom you should address your letter. If the ad states, "No phone calls," call the main number for the company and ask the name of the employment manager. Don't indicate that you are responding to an advertisement. If the ad uses a blind box response ("send resume to Box XXXX"), and you can't even determine the company name, that usually means the incumbent in the position does not know he or she is being replaced. In those cases, address your letter as stated, and then use, "Dear Employment Manager," as a salutation.

3. Take some words or phrases directly from the advertisement and use them in your letter.

4. Don't rehash what's already in your resume. The trick is to highlight or amplify specific qualifications.

5. Anticipate objections. If you are missing a stated qualification for the position, offer an offsetting advantage. Give them some explanation of how you can do the job despite not having something they are seeking. They are going to match your resume, item for item, against the qualifications anyway. If you don't have it, tell them that what you do have is even better than what they want.

6. Tell them not what you hope to gain but what you are going to give.

7. Regardless of what the ad requests, never give the company your salary requirements or your current income.

Income is used as a quick disqualifier. If you are too high in your present income, employers will assume you are overqualified, that the job is really beneath you, and you will quickly become disenchanted. If you are too low, they'll assume you are not qualified for such a big jump in salary, and the job would be more than you can handle. In general, wait for the interview or, at the very earliest, the pre-interview arrangements to begin discussing salary.

Example Letter of Transmittal Responding to the Previous Ad

12 Street of Dreams
Woods, MO 43222

January 17, 1993

Mr. Frank Hardnose
XYZ Nut Fastener Company
P.O. Box 5555
Podunk, IL 66606

Dear Mr. Hardnose:

I am responding to your advertisement in the *Podunk Sunday Sun* on January 15, for the position of high speed yo-yo operator.

I noted in your advertisement that you are seeking an individual who is suave, debonair, and devil-may-care. As you review my resume, you will note that I not only have the qualifications and abilities that you are seeking, but additionally I have seven years of progressively responsible experience in the yo-yo field. My management background includes both training and hands-on experience supervising up to seventeen yo-yo crew members. Although I do not have a bachelors degree, I have an extensive background as a trainer and troubleshooter in career positions spanning over fifteen years.

Please call me at your earliest convenience at (303) 444-4444 to arrange a time when we can get together for an interview.

Thank you very much.

Sincerely,

Joseph D. Ragman

Enclosure

As you can see, the letter of transmittal gets right to the heart of what you are trying to do. It tells the employer where you saw the ad and what position you are applying for, and it lists the qualifications for the job as your own abilities. It shows interest and offers an offsetting advantage for a stated but missing qualification. Finally, it tells the potential employer you are expecting an interview. As you can see, this letter of transmittal differs dramatically from the usual cover letter.

Response to a Personal Lead.   If a friend, colleague, or acquaintance suggested you write a particular person to inquire about employment, then refer to the lead's name in the first sentence. For example:

> I was talking with our mutual friend, Bill Johnson, yesterday. He suggested I write to you to inquire about my possible affiliation with Acme Widgets. . . .

Mass Mailings.   Do mass mailings work? Of course they do. For years we helped prepare thousands of cover letters for job seekers all over the country, and our colleagues at Word Store in Charlottesville, Virginia, continue that work. The kind of response these job seekers get depends on the product they're selling. Certainly people with little experience and little strength in their resumes cannot expect a very good response. But those with good experience and good credentials can and do get results.

What kind of response? That also depends on their market. Some professions grant many interviews as a result of mail solicitations. In the legal profession, for example, most law firms do not have sophisticated recruiting systems. Most law firms in this country have fewer than ten members. They don't have the time or resources to devote to recruiting. Their needs can appear suddenly. At any given time, then, some percentage of all law firms is looking for a new associate.

The same is true of most professions and businesses. Most professional firms and businesses are small and do not have sophisticated recruiting systems. At any time, even in the depths of a recession, a percentage of employers is looking for employees. Next week or next month the percentage will probably be the same. The identity of those looking is unknown. Each week or each month the identity of those looking will change. Someone who was looking last month isn't looking now. Someone who wasn't looking last month is looking now. Direct mail efficiently and quickly seeks out those who are looking.

So what kind of response can you expect? About 1 to 2 percent, if you're lucky. Ask anybody who has marketed goods and services by direct mail. All they expect is 1 to 2 percent. The best we've ever done selling through direct mail is 6 percent. The worst, predictably, is 0 percent. But there is one cardinal rule in direct mail, one absolute certainty: Every letter you don't send will not result in an interview, and every letter you do send might result in an interview. It's a numbers game. Does it work? Ask the young professional woman who sent out more than 1,000 letters. She got better than a 2 percent response, and more than twenty interviews. In three weeks flat she began her new job making $12,000 more than she was making before. Or ask the young liberal arts student who sent out 300 letters to large corporations. After just one month he had the precise job he wanted in Houston.

Getting an Address List.   Use the target list you developed from your library research in directories and trade publications. Many of these directories will have the names of executive officers. You should, of course, write to employment managers. Watch for the titles *vice president of personnel* or *vice president of human resources.* If you know the exact kind of position you seek, you should also write the executive in your field. If you want an advertising job, write to the vice president of public relations or of marketing. If you want a sales position, locate the executive whose title reveals a direct interest in sales. The same holds for computer positions, editorial positions, or any other job: try to identify the person who might end up being your ultimate boss. If you can identify both the recruiter and the ultimate boss, include both on your address list. Send a separate letter to each. If you cannot identify a person, you're stuck with addressing your letters to the personnel office and using the salutation, "Dear Sir or Madam."

How Many Letters to Send.   With mass mailings you're just looking for a 1 to 2 percent favorable response rate. This is the same level of response anyone in marketing will seek with direct mail advertising. We know the response sounds terrible, but think about what you are selling. How much do you cost? If you're looking for a $20,000 job to last about five years, then you cost $100,000 plus all the overhead needed to give you a place to work. If you're looking for a $50,000 job for five years, then you're selling a $250,000 item. A 1 to 2 percent response rate for that kind of sale is wonderful.

Consider this, too. Why do car advertisers keep running ads all the time? Why not just run a few several times each year? The reason is that at any given moment a certain percentage of all people are in the market for a new car. To guarantee a maximum return on the advertising dollar the car manufacturers hit the market all the time. Are they really trying to convince someone who just bought a car to buy another? No. They're going after those who are beginning to think about buying a new car. They're going after that small percentage who are ripe for a sale.

So, too, in the business of selling yourself. At any given moment a certain percentage of employers need new people for the exact kind of job you want. If you could magically determine exactly which employers are ripe for a sale, then you'd just send your letters to them. But you don't know which employers make up that small percentage right now. To maximize the return on your advertising dollar you must send as many letters as you can afford.

Remember, every letter you don't send will definitely result in no interview. Every letter you do send has a 2 percent chance of yielding an interview. You hope to get about two interviews for every 100 letters you send out. Also, if you send out twice as many letters, you'll get twice as many interviews—and twice as many rejections.

Personalizing Your Cover Letters

With today's modern word processing technology you can create a single letter and send it to hundreds of addressees. Each one looks, in effect, individually typed. Each one looks personal. But does it sound personal? Ideally you would prepare a letter individually written and tailored to each person on your address list. Each letter would sound highly personal. But such a project would be prohibitively expensive and time consuming.

At least you can try to tailor your set letter to each addressee by having your word processing program insert variables within the body of your letter. Each letter should have a personal salutation, "Dear Mr. Smith" or "Dear Ms. Thompson." But you can go further than this by variably inserting the name of the company and the name of the city or state. As you copy down your address list during your directory research, write down the most likely company organization nickname for each addressee. The nickname will frequently be quite obvious. International Business Machines, Inc., is IBM. The Coca-Cola Bottling Company is Coca-Cola (not Coke). The Securities and Exchange Commission is the SEC. Other nicknames won't be so obvious. You'll have to take a reasonable chance. Try to surmise how the people working for that company would refer to it in general conversation. For example, a company named International Widgets Consolidated, Inc., is probably nicknamed International Widgets. Typically you can figure it out.

In the body of your letter you can have your word processing program insert the name of the company. But you don't want that insertion to read like this:

> I think you'll agree I can bring a wealth of experience to International Widgets Consolidated, Inc.

That's the way it will read if your program is instructed to insert the company name from the inside address field. Instead, you want the body of the letter to read:

> I think you'll agree I can bring a wealth of experience to International Widgets.

So you'll need a company nickname for you or the word processing operator to input for each name and address.

You can play other tricks with inserting the state or city in the body of the letter. Suppose you plan to take an interview trip to several cities in the Northeast. If you don't insert the city name, your letter would have to read like this:

> I'll be in your area during the week of June 1–7 and will welcome the chance to meet you personally.

But you can instruct your word processing machine to insert the city name for each addressee so the letter will read like this for the Boston letters:

> I'll be in Boston during the week of June 1–7 and will welcome the chance to meet you personally.

And like this for the New York letters:

> I'll be in New York during the week of June 1–7 and will welcome the chance to meet you personally.

If you overdo it with variable insertions, you'll defeat your purpose. Mention the company's name once and no more than twice. Follow the same rule for cities and states. Also, do not insert the addressee's name in the body of the letter. Don't write:

> Once again, Mr. Jones, I appreciate your taking the time to review my credentials.

Restrict the name insertion to the personalized salutation, "Dear Mr. Jones." Otherwise you'll end up sounding like one of those form letters that say:

> Well, how is the Jones family today sitting there in your home at 101 Main Street in Peoria, Illinois?

Supplies and Production

When your resume is prepared, be sure to obtain a supply of blank pages and envelopes made from the same paper stock as your resume. Your cover letters should be prepared using the same type as your resume. To produce these letters most effectively, you will need a personal computer and high-quality printer. Use a letter-quality printer or a laser printer with a resolution of 300 dots per inch. An alternative is to use a first-class electric typewriter. If all else fails, you can probably find a secretarial service that will help you for a fee. Check around. Draft the letters and then have them typed in batches each week.

One final touch. Go to the post office and buy some commemorative stamps for your letters. We don't know why, but in every test we've done on direct mail, those letters sent with commemorative stamps always yield a better response.

The All-Important Follow-Up

Remember, there are only three ways to tell people you are available for a job. First, you can call them on the telephone. Second, you can visit them in person. Third, you can send them a letter.

The final part of prospecting is the follow-up. At this stage of the game, you've only sent a letter. Now it's time to hound on the phone or in person. Sending the letter and the resume does not end your responsibility. You don't just sit back and wait for the phone to ring. Up to this point, every action you have taken has been on paper. You really have not had any personal contact with employers.

If you have not received a response to your letter of transmittal within two weeks, from any employer or for any position you consider a good prospect, you should follow up with a personal telephone call. Try to reach the exact person who received your letter; don't be satisfied with leaving a message with the receptionist of the human resources office or the secretary of the employment manager. Tell the employment manager you are checking to ensure the letter was received because you are very interested in employment with that company. This will cause the manager at least to pull your letter and resume out and check to see your name on it. The only reason for the call is for the person involved to see your name and, you hope, to place your resume on the top of the pile. Don't be pushy or cute when you call. Merely say you are checking on the mail system, expressing your interest in the position, and asking when they expect to begin interviews. The call should be very professional, very brief, and should end on a positive note, such as, "Thanks for checking for me. I am looking forward to hearing from you soon."

Prospecting in Numbers

Prospecting can and will get you interviews, but to be effective it should be multifaceted and include as many leads and sources as you can develop. Look for every opportunity and then go after each with a letter, a resume, and a follow-up call. Try not to get discouraged if you are not immediately successful, or if you don't get an interview with every attempt. Prospecting is another numbers game. To be successful you have to get lots more leads than you will ever wrap up. A job seeker recently told us he sent out almost 100 resumes and got only one interview. If he had sent out 200 letters, he would have received two interviews. If he had sent out 1,000 letters, he would have received ten interviews. The more letters you send, the more contact you make, the more rejections you'll receive, but the more positive responses you'll receive as well.

Focus, But Blast Away

Imagine a hunter who is going after birds. The hunter uses a shotgun that fires a large load of pellets. He knows it only takes one pellet to bring down his target, but he fires the large load because he doesn't know which pellet will hit. If he knew, he would have to fire only one. The message here is that although he fires a large load, he fires them all in the same direction.

The same theory applies to the job search. You are going to be firing letters and resumes into the job market in large numbers, hoping one will get you the interview that will land you the great job you want. Be careful to fire them all in the same direction. Don't dilute your efforts and make your marketing plan less effective. For you, the target is not a bird on the wing, but that goal of money, location, or job that you originally established for yourself. There's no sense in prospecting for traveling sales jobs in Pittsburgh when what you really want is a marketing management position in New York.

Doing What Everybody Else Doesn't

Finally, to become an expert prospector, it's a good idea to realize that thousands of other people are prospecting too, looking for the same gold, in the same territory, using the same techniques. Scads of other people are sending out resumes (lousy ones, you hope) and pre-printed run-of-the-mill cover letters. Your job is to be different, to do what everybody else does not do. Everybody else sends boring cover letters, so you send a letter of transmittal. Everybody else has professionally prepared resumes, so you do your own. Everybody else sends letters in a business envelope, so you use a nine-by-twelve envelope so your letter and resume arrive unfolded. Everybody else uses regular postage stamps, so you get a supply of commemorative stamps. Everybody else just responds to classified ads, so you respond to classified ads, launch a direct mail campaign, write letters to the authors of articles, call up old friends in your newly discovered network, read professional or trade journals, make telephone calls, and make personal visits.

Figure out what everybody else doesn't do, and then do that. That's the way to get a job. Indeed, that's the way to succeed in almost everything you do.

CHAPTER 10

Help!

And Where to Find It

GETTING HELP WITH YOUR job search or career transition rarely is a problem. Getting the right help often is. As soon as you let friends, family, and colleagues know about your quest, you're sure to receive plenty of free advice, including critiques of your resume. An important part of your job is to persist in looking for help until you find sources that really do help you sell your product as you have defined it. If you find out later that you had some misconceptions about yourself or your qualifications, or actually want or need something different from what you first thought you wanted, your response to that new understanding should be a considered, thoughtful reevaluation, following a process similar to the one given earlier in this book. It should not be a disorganized, impulsive, emotional retreat. In other words, don't let sudden gusts of advice or a few cold blasts of discouragement change your mind. If you change your mind, be certain you're the one who's changing it. It's all too easy to let yourself fall or be pushed from your goal into whatever someone else thinks is better or more reasonable.

What you need is help that truly helps, not help that pushes or pulls. Once you find true help, you'll know it. Here are some places to look.

Agencies

If you're just looking for a job, one of your first stops should be the state employment service. If you're more concerned about getting the right job for your career, then the state agencies will be farther down on your list. If you've been let go from your previous position, of course, you might be eligible for unemployment benefits, so be sure to inquire to determine your eligibility.

Private employment agencies are potentially a great source of help. An employment agency can be anything from a firm that places mostly entry-level and clerical personnel all the way to something like a headhunter or executive search organization. Distinctions between different types or classes of agencies have been melting in recent years, with some so-called employment agencies placing executives in the top ranks of major corporations. Both employment agencies and executive search firms advertise in the yellow pages, major metropolitan area Sunday newspapers, and trade journals. The best source of information concerning agencies, however, is probably word of mouth; if you can, find out how people who are doing the kind of work you seek got their jobs.

Agencies tend to be more important in large metropolitan markets, where you can find firms that place applicants in jobs at every level; they also operate nationally in specialized fields and for jobs at the executive level. They are not for everybody or for all situations. There are many reasons why an employment agency might not be the best avenue for you. Perhaps you're looking for a job in a small town, for example, or the firms you're interested in handle all their employment through their personnel office, or the company that's best for you is a small start-up operation that doesn't want to pay agency fees.

On the other hand, if you find the right employment agency for you and your field, it can be a shortcut to a good job. A good employment counselor can become not only a valuable advisor but your spoken resume. The counselor can help make up for the inflexibility of having a resume that might not fit some of the opportunities you'd like to pursue; he or she becomes the equivalent of your personal computer, the one you'd use to revise your objective and change the order of entries for that job. The counselor often will pitch you to the employer and try to get you an interview before the employer has even seen your resume.

If you're extremely well qualified for the work you want, a good agency can often help you get where you're going faster than anyone else. The top agencies in a given field know which companies are hot and which ones have resources, if only because they know which ones are doing well enough to be able to afford the sizeable agency fees. (If you're hired, the agency charges the hiring company in the range of one-third of your annual salary as the fee for having referred you.) They are intimately familiar with the companies they serve and know which ones are really committed to the projects they're hiring for and which ones are likely to suffer from freezes and cutbacks. An agency in a particular field or specialty will see the person they placed in a company several years later when she comes back looking for a new job; they may hear from someone at the top level of another company when he calls to test the market. Little by little, they can assemble a very accurate picture of what's happening in their industry. And there are agencies for just about every industry, profession, and niche you can imagine —agencies that place nothing but editors and executives for publishing houses and magazines, agencies for accountants, agencies whose exclusive province is placing staffers from dishwashers to social directors for resort hotels in places like the Catskill Mountains.

You should research the agencies near where you'll be working—or if you're at the executive level or have highly specialized professional skills, check with your library for a national directory that will guide you to the appropriate agency, which may be in another part of the country. One excellent source is the *Directory of Executive Recruiters* ($44.95 for the 1993 edition from Kennedy Publications, Templeton Road, Fitzwilliam, NH 03447, 1-800-531-0007; VISA and MasterCard accepted). This book has contact information on hundreds of executive search firms and some good ideas on how you can use them to help in your job search.

Getting Your Name on File

When you visit agencies, you'll fill out their job-history forms as well as submit your resume. If the agency is in another town, send them your resume and request their form so that they'll have you on file. Talk with the counselors and ask them to review your resume and your salary expectations for that marketplace. See if they think they can get you some interviews.

When approaching employment agencies, keep in mind where you stand in their scheme of things. The agency's primary role is to serve the hiring company, which is the source of the agency's income. In most cases, the difficult challenge for an agency is to find company clients and job listings; it's not nearly as difficult for them to find good applicants. Therefore, when dealing with agencies it's smart to remember that you really can't demand service beyond a certain level of fairness, because you don't have that kind of leverage—just by virtue of being one of many applicants. You might not get the red-carpet treatment from an agency when you apply. Perhaps your background doesn't match the kinds of positions this particular agency is used to filling, or perhaps they haven't got anything for you at that time.

If an agency doesn't seem to want to work with you, don't break your back. Any employment counselor will tell you placing your name and background before a hiring company is not exactly strenuous work, so, generally speaking, if an agency sees a way to try to place you, it will. No one in an agency is going to throw money away knowingly, and if you're a viable candidate for a $35,000 job, for example, you have a $10,000 value to some agency. So consider what recourse you have: you either need to find an agency that needs what you offer in order to fill its positions, you need to enhance your value through some further experience or special training, or you need to do without agencies. Again, it's vital to research the agencies to see if you can find one that's right for you, one that will work with you based on your value. And remember that their perception of your value may depend in part on your ability to present that value in a resume.

Beware

As in any field, you need to be careful of unscrupulous people who may try to place you in a job just to get their fee, even though that job may not be at all what you want or need and may not be in your best interest. Agents everywhere know of dead-end jobs that keep coming back as listings year after year; some agents won't care if they place you in such a position, as long as they get their fee, which they will as long as you stay employed in that job a certain number of weeks.

The story of one homemaker who was returning to the job market in New York illustrates this danger as well as the wisdom of taking action to upgrade your value, if necessary. She wanted an editorial secretary's job in publishing, in a location that would not require a long commute. She was told right away she was unemployable because she didn't have experience working with personal computers. However, one agency was only too happy to refer her to a job—a dead-end, often-vacated clerical job with a small financial firm in Wall Street, a long commute from her home. The temptation to take this job was strong, but she refused to let herself be pushed. For $250 she took a one-week course in WordPerfect and Lotus 1-2-3, emerged more proficient than some people who have used these programs for years, re-applied at other agencies, and soon had an editorial secretary's job at one of the nation's top magazines, within walking distance from her apartment.

Who Pays the Fee?

We don't recommend that you pay anyone to help you find work. It's not especially fair for an agency to charge you as well as collect fees from clients. In addition, never give anyone an exclusive contract on you. You want as many sources as possible working for you. Don't sign any contract unless you read every word. Some agencies use deceptive advertising to get you in the door, but don't, in fact, serve as an outplacement agency with specific job vacancy listings. This has been identified as a real problem in the employment industry, so be careful.

College Placement Office (Even If You're No Longer a Student)

If you are now in school, by all means take advantage of the array of resources offered by your university placement and career planning offices. If you're out of school, perhaps you took it for granted that when you graduated from your alma mater, its services were no longer available to you. In the case of placement and career planning, that may not be true. And if you've been away from college for a long while—twelve years or more—you may not realize the potential resource you have in your old school's placement and career planning offices. Those functions have grown tremendously in importance since you left. Placement and career planning offices have become key helpers for a growing percentage of students and for many alumni.

How They Work

The placement and career planning offices at our colleges and universities are all different. So when you consider how to use a placement office, you'll need to check first to see what kinds of services might be available. In some schools, one main office handles both career counseling and job placement for most students and alumni. Thus career counseling and planning, job-search information and strategies, and placement are all available under one roof. (However, most professional schools within universities—such as medical, law, and graduate business schools—have their own placement offices.) In this setup, the school's counseling center usually does very little career-planning work, but instead helps students with emotional, social, and academic problems.

In other schools, the counseling center is also responsible for career planning, and, as such, holds the library dealing with occupations. Yet the placement office may have the information about resume-writing and job-hunting. Thus placement and career counseling are split. Another variation in big universities is decentralized placement, so that each major school or division has its own placement office, with career counseling available somewhere else. Many smaller colleges put everything in one office, so that students who are depressed, students who are try-ing to develop study skills, students who are trying to figure out what career to pursue, and students and alumni who are looking for jobs all go to the same place.

Will They Work with Alumni?

College placement and career counseling offices differ widely in their willingness or mission to work with alumni. Some simply don't do it. Others are explicitly committed to working with students at any time throughout their lives, even if their focus naturally is strongest on the years students are at school. Alumni can come to the offices and use their services, or call in for assistance. Still other schools have developed special ser-vices for alumni, including forms of outreach such as career workshops in major cities away from the campus location.

Here are some examples from a large state university of what a school's placement office can do for its graduates:

A young woman one year out of school, who had taken a job with a Pennsylvania company through on-campus recruiting, has left her job and is hoping to find work in Washington. Her placement office helps her with several of her important ques-tions: How do I job-hunt in Washington? Can you look at my resume and tell me if it needs changes? Whom should I con-tact? Can you coach me on interview skills? She uses the of-fice's library resources to identify employers, to identify alumni who might be key contacts, and to look at company literature for information about specific employers.

Another visitor to the office, an alumnus who has been in the Navy for four years since his graduation, has never before used the placement office. Now he wants to use his double major in computer science and psychology, plus his Navy experience, to find work in artificial intelligence. The office helps him develop a resume that communicates his objective, shows his skills, and describes his military experience in terms that make sense to private employers. The office helps him identify likely employers and coaches him on how to approach them.

This placement office is accustomed to seeing alumni who graduated within the past few years, but it would also be receptive to someone who had graduated twenty or more years ago and was looking for a career change. Then there are schools, usually in large urban areas, whose placement and career counseling offices regularly see alumni of every stripe and vintage, who in fact work more with alumni than with students because the great majority of their alumni stay in the metropolitan area. The student population itself at some of these schools is nontraditional, with many undergraduates older than twenty-one, such as military personnel returning to school, returning homemakers, and professionals switching careers. If you're from this kind of school, or if you simply live or work near one, the same advice applies: see how its placement office can help you.

Long-Distance Help

If you're too far from your school to visit, its placement office may still be able to help you. See if they have a newsletter or other mailing giving their latest job vacancy listings. Such listings are often old by the time you've received them, so you might instead call and inquire about listings. While you're at it, have them send you any handouts they have on topics relevant to your search, as well as a list, if available, of other alumni in your area, or the area to which you're moving, who have indicated their willingness to act as contacts.

A great alternative to conventional published listings is the job hotline, a service available at some schools that students or alumni can register for, although its greatest usefulness tends to be for alumni. When you register, you indicate the geographic area you want, and the kind of work you're looking for—journalism in the Baltimore area, for example, or marketing management in Florida. You can then call any time on a touch-tone phone into the hotline and get a voice recording of vacancies that match your criteria, telling you whom to get in touch with and what you need to send. Basically, you're getting a classified ad over the phone, with the advantage of being able to get the listing almost as soon as it comes into the placement

office. Another possible advantage: some schools are networking their systems with other universities, giving you access to
listings from several schools.

What They Offer

Listings. Virtually all placement offices have job listings. (See
our discussion of listings and job hotlines above.) At some
schools, anyone can come in to the placement or career planning office and consult any of the resources that are posted or
out on the shelves, attend workshops, or use computer databases
and programs. This can be good news if you're in a city far away
from your alma mater, for you might be able to gain access to
schools in your area. Some universities will card you at the door,
and others will say they won't let you use the library without
a letter of reciprocity from your school. But it's well worth trying, because even if they turn you away, people in the placement field are trained to be helpers; they may refer you to
another place that can help you.

Even if you're working with your old school's placement
office, be sure to check placement offices in the area where
you're job-hunting, if only for the job listings. Those listings
will probably be more complete and more current for your region
than the ones provided at a distance by your school.

Counseling. All career planning offices offer one-to-one counseling; many will see alumni. Counseling might be on any of
a variety of issues from resume writing to what to do if you hate
your job. Many offices, especially those with large numbers of
alumni living in the area, offer group counseling or workshops
to deal with some of the same issues.

Library. The libraries in placement and career planning offices
vary dramatically, but if your school's office has a good one, it
may prove to be your best hunting ground for resources and information, and an even better place to start your job search than
a main university library. A good placement or career counseling

library (see "How They Work" on page 198) will have directories for many different types of employment, literature from employers, job-search books, general career information, books on specific career areas, and information about cost of living and salaries.

The placement or career planning library is a good starting point for you if only because so many related resources are likely to be accessible in one place. At a main university or civic library these sources are scattered, and you have to know what you're looking for. The placement library staff can usually tell you if they're missing something that the university library has, such as a more recent edition of a directory you're interested in consulting.

Resume Help. Almost all placement or career planning offices can offer you at least some resume-writing assistance. A big advantage of that over private sources is that the help is often free. Some schools do charge fees for alumni to use any of their services, but the fees are usually small compared to those charged by resume-writing businesses. As we said in Chapter 3, be sure you supervise the choice of headings and the basic content any time you have someone else produce your resume.

Contacts. Most placement offices will be able to provide you with employer contacts and alumni contacts. These might appear in the form of directories or simply a list of people the counselor knows. Some schools have done a tremendous job of arranging for alumni to help both current students and other alumni. Among the strengths of smaller schools often are their alumni networks.

Testing. Placement offices usually offer tests that may be required by major employers; many offer the CIA and NSA tests and the Foreign Service Exams. Career planning offices typically also offer interest inventories and personality tests that can help you define your interests and evaluate potential careers. These tests often cost a lot more at private centers than at many career planning offices. Computer-assisted guidance programs are also available which, like the interest testing, allow you to respond to questions about what's important to you, what you're good at, and what you enjoy doing; you typically then get a list of careers based on your answers. The programs often include an occupational database so that you can ask questions about the true nature of the career you're interested in.

Besides guidance software, other computer programs frequently available include databases for job vacancies in state and federal government, private employer databases, and software that can guide you through resume writing.

Workshops.   Interview workshops are offered by most placement offices, and in many cases alumni may attend. Some schools also will conduct mock interviews with anybody who wants one. The procedure is usually to make an appointment with a counselor and submit a resume along with the job description of the position you wish to be interviewed for, to give the staff time to prepare for the role of employer.

You may also find resume-writing workshops, workshops on how to get a job in a particular major city, workshops on how to dress for interviews, and even workshops on etiquette to teach you how to deal with the forks and spoons and introductions in a business dinner. Some offices will have videos available on these subjects. Some will even stage an interview with a recruiter and a student live, for an audience.

Credentials.   Most career planning and placement offices have some kind of credentials service. Although this service is most often needed to help collect and file letters of recommendation for graduate school, it can also be of help in certain kinds of job searches.

Formal letters of recommendation for most kinds of jobs are on the way out simply because employers have become wary of the basic to-whom-it-may-concern, Jane-Doe-is-a-great-person document. Most placement offices encourage job hunters, just as we have done earlier in this book, to submit the names, titles, addresses, and telephone numbers of their references along with their resumes, either on first submission or as a follow-up when the employer expresses interest. Written letters are better when they pertain to a specific job you're seeking. However, letters of recommendation are still important for Ph.D.'s seeking teaching or research positions, for education school graduates, and for nurses; many placement offices will help you collect and keep track of these letters if you need them.

Job Fairs.   Job fairs are a popular way for placement offices to bring employers together with students and alumni. These often have special themes, and some are tailored for alumni. At alumni career fairs, occasionally staged for a school's alumni in a particular metropolitan area, employers each have a table, and alumni come by to talk and submit resumes. Sometimes employers set up interviews based on that brief contact. They usually don't interview at the job fair, although some fairs are structured so that the first day (or morning) features contact, and the second day (afternoon) allows interviews.

If you're from a small liberal arts college, job fairs can go a long way toward making up for any weakness in the school's appeal to employers. Small colleges in the same region sometimes work together to stage job or career fairs, which attract employers by bringing students and alumni from several schools to one event.

On-Campus Recruiting.   Almost all schools offer some kind of campus recruiting, in which employers come on campus to interview students or alumni for jobs. Some schools will not allow alumni to participate. In any event, it can be difficult for you to participate if you're not living near the campus. It might not make sense to job-hunt this way if, for example, you're working in New York and want to get in touch with a New York employer; there's probably no advantage in traveling to your old campus in Rhode Island or Georgia to contact that company when you can do it on the employer's own turf.

Although the on-campus interview season works in different ways at different schools, a few generalities tend to hold true. Employers who take advantage of on-campus recruiting tend to be in the areas of big business and big government agencies, as well as medium-size to large companies from the school's geographic region. Most employers who recruit on college campuses need to do a substantial amount of hiring and are big enough that they can predict their needs months in advance; they may be going to campuses to interview in October knowing they will hire sixty engineers, or thirty management trainees, to start in June.

A large school might have over a dozen employers interviewing on campus every day from October to April. Although this sounds as though it makes for a fabulous abundance of opportunity, you should be aware of the limitations of on-campus recruiting. For example, among employers typically not represented in on-campus recruiting are virtually all small businesses, which are tremendous sources of job opportunities. These are not the kinds of organizations that find on-campus recruiting to be cost-effective. Advertising agencies, newspapers, radio stations, publishing houses, social service agencies, hospitals— these are just a sampling of types of employers usually not represented on-campus recruiting.

Organizations also tend to recruit on campus for the kinds of jobs for which they need people in substantial numbers, such as engineers, financial analysts, marketing and sales people, bank management trainees, management consultants, programmers, and systems analysts. These employers generally do not come to interview for personnel people, public relations trainees, designers, or many other kinds of employees, even though they may indeed need these people. Therefore if you're interested in a company that is coming to your school, and you're interested in personnel, for example, that employer might not talk to you about personnel jobs during on-campus recruiting. You may have to approach that company at its offices.

That doesn't mean, however, that you shouldn't try to talk with that company while they're at your campus. Call and talk to them before they come, write them a letter, or meet them on campus while they're taking a break.

Here's how on-campus recruiting works at a number of schools. Employers tell the placement office what kinds of candidates they're interested in. The placement office relays the information to you, the participant, in a book or schedule that lists the company, contact person, address, phone number (so that you can write to the employment manager directly if you wish), and a date for collection of resumes. The placement office bundles your resume with all the others submitted for that company and sends them to the company's employment manager so that he or she can decide whom to interview.

The employment manager might get 300 resumes from that school and might be sending two recruiters to the campus for one day. Out of these the employment manager's going to pick perhaps twenty-six, expecting to fit in thirteen interviews per day. Resumes, again, are critical: If you don't stand out on that piece of paper, you probably won't get an interview.

At many schools the process will have begun with orientation meetings to explain the logistics to students who will be graduating. Attendance at a meeting may be a prerequisite to obtaining the ticket you'll need for the recruiting schedules.

On-campus interviews normally don't culminate in a job offer. They are screening interviews, half an hour long. Generally if you do well in this interview you'll get a letter or phone call inviting you for another interview at the company, at their expense. One advantage of on-campus recruiting, then, is that it gives you access to employers from all over at no expense, with the possibility that you may get to travel to places where you might be interested in working, also at no expense. If you're doing an independent job search and haven't had a campus interview, and you're getting in touch with an organization in another city, it's unlikely they'll pay your way to come out for an interview, especially if you're a recent college graduate.

Do I Have to Be Corporate Material?

These days, a majority of students use the placement and career counseling offices. A misperception lingers at large universities, however, that the placement office is there to help business majors and engineers, not the liberal arts student. This comes about because the most visible career-related activity at many schools is campus recruiting, during which the office may be flooded by people in three-piece suits. That's an image many placement offices have made a conscious effort to overcome. Even though a majority of business and engineering students at many schools do get their jobs through on-campus recruiting, many other students get jobs that way and, more to the point, get jobs and job-search help in other ways through the placement office.

For Students Only

If you're currently a student, there are several key ways your placement office can help you before you're ready to find that first job after graduation. Here are some of them:

Summer Jobs and Internships.   The placement office can help you find summer jobs. These include the usual sorts of jobs, such as waiting tables, whose appeal is primarily money. Placement offices usually have directories of jobs available in resort areas and camps, for example, which can help you out.

Placement offices may be more highly motivated, though, to help you find a summer internship related to your career goals. The larger and more active placement offices work hard to develop internships, jobs in your area of interest where you can serve in an apprentice or helper capacity, to learn about the field and test your career goals. Here the appeal of the position isn't money but experience. Internships in social services and government, for example, are most often either unpaid or low paying. Business internships are well paid, but the intern's goal is nevertheless to gain experience (and valuable contacts). Internships can be in glamorous settings in major cities, such as on Capitol Hill, on Wall Street, or in media, or they can be right in front of your nose—writing and producing publicity, for example, for your school's placement office. Your placement office may have entire directories of internships in different metropolitan areas and in different fields, from media to finance.

Applying for an internship is practically identical to the process of applying for permanent career-related jobs. You need a resume, you need interviews, you need this book, none of which you would need to apply for a job waiting tables at the beach. The internship gives you early experience in the career job-search process.

Externships.   An externship is a mini-internship, a one-week volunteer opportunity to test a field you think you might be interested in. If you think you want to be an account executive in advertising, your placement office might be able to send you to an advertising firm to shadow an account executive for a week. Because it's one week, you might not get significant experience. The main purpose is to see what goes on, by shadowing someone who's doing what you think you'd like to do, by observing, and by asking questions.

Not every placement office is going to have an externship program. But where programs have been developed, they've become important tools for helping students launch career searches. Placement offices will often ask you to research what you want to do and where you'd like to go for an externship, and the office will try to arrange it.

The externship can also be a kind of week-long interview, which sometimes leads to a summer internship or even a permanent job, thanks to contacts you've made.

Courses.   Many placement and career planning offices offer courses for credit. These include types of career-planning seminars, which immerse you in thinking about what you want to do, who you are, and what you're good at, and which require you to research careers of interest to you.

Other common course offerings, usually for graduating students, concern the job search: resume writing, employer identification, interviewing, networking. Extra benefits of these courses are that you meet other people who are facing the same questions you're facing, and you're forced to take needed steps that you might not otherwise get around to taking.

Guides and Directories.   If you need to decide where your talents lie or what career field you can enter, there are many publications that can help you to focus your direction. The *Occupational Outlook Handbook,* published by the U.S. Department of Labor, provides general information on various career fields including qualifications for entry, earning potential, and future needs in the economy for the skill. The *Directory of Career Training and Development Programs*, published by the Ready Reference Press, lists companies and business organizations offering professional training and internship programs in business, retailing, finance, hospitality, and other industries. They also publish the *Directory of Internships, Work Experience Programs and On the Job Training Opportunities*. This can give you good ideas. Another good source is *The Career Guide* published by Duns Marketing Services.

A Book, a Mirror—How About a Candle?

A very wise and experienced professional in the career-placement field once told us the problem with giving advice in print is that readers pick up on whatever appeals to them, but can't find in the printed pages the one thing they most need to see: themselves. Our checklist in Chapter 1 is designed to help reflect to you the qualities you have that employers are seeking. Most of the rest of what we have said is to aid you in projecting those qualities to employers, in the form of your resume and, later, the interview. But since this book cannot be an all-purpose magic mirror, we can perhaps best serve your interests by suggesting that you be alert to the mirrors that help you the most in your search. Usually this means finding a mentor of some kind; it could be anyone, a personal friend, a banker, a therapist, a healer or physician, a guidance counselor, your grandmother. Having a few trusted sources of advice means you won't run around following everyone's, or just anyone's, advice. Instead you'll stick with counsel from someone who knows you and mirrors yourself to you, with fidelity and with an image in mind of you at your best. Given the basic tools we have developed here, a sound foundation of knowledge about the job search, and a structure for how to present yourself, such a mentor can be the light that guides you to the fulfilling work you want and deserve.

CHAPTER 11

Your Product Demonstration

The Interview

YOU'VE INVESTED A LOT of time and effort to get to this point in the job search. You have researched, written, prospected, and planned with the single goal of obtaining an interview. Your search reflects your self-confidence. Confidence is important, and it will help you in presenting your qualifications, but you aren't going to beat out the competition with confidence alone. Interviewing is a complex process that requires careful planning, an organized approach, and a good measure of rehearsal. In this chapter you'll gain some insights into the tricky process of the interview so that you don't wind up getting ambushed on the final path to success.

The purpose of the interview is to allow you to present your qualifications. The interview is not an office visit or a friendly conversation, but an exchange of views and ideas between you and the interviewer in which your qualifications will be matched against the requirements for the job. It is the interviewer's responsibility to control and guide the interview toward that goal. You also have some responsibilities. You must ensure the interviewer gets enough information to make a decision, and you must listen to ensure you answer each question completely. It is also your responsibility to stay on track.

Clothes

Your first step in getting ready for the interview is to get yourself into the proper uniform. There is a uniform in corporate America, and in other employment settings, and you really have to comply with the dress standards. If you doubt that, pick up a copy of the annual report of any major company that includes photographs of the executives or the board of directors. See how they are dressed. Those are the people who set the standards for the company. The first rule for interviewing is to remember that the interviewer will judge your appearance based on his or her standards, not yours! It doesn't matter what your impression of stylishness may be. It's the interviewer's standards of taste that matter most.

So your first task is to do some further research. There are some excellent books on the subject of dress, such as *Dress for Success*. But the best way to find out about dress standards is to go and look. Visit a place where you will find business people in your industry. What you will generally see are people who dress conservatively, and who all dress alike. You might find that the people in your industry do not dress formally. For example, if you seek a position that requires you to work with your hands, such as an equipment operator or a mechanic, don't show up for the interview in a suit. The employer will feel you might not be willing to get in there and get your hands dirty. On the other hand, don't show up in blue jeans, sneakers, and a t-shirt.

Some positions and situations, and some types of firms, may call for a degree of informality for the interview somewhere between those of the manual worker and the business executive. Examples include interviews for graphic artists, computer software designers, writers, and other creative positions. Here there's more leeway, although it's still important to project a reassuring, responsible image. In other words, don't take dumb risks with your wardrobe, and be sensitive to the culture of the industry and even of the particular firm.

You should be able to put together an interview wardrobe for a minimum amount of money. There are many discount clothing stores around if you watch for sales, for both men and women. But if you're faced with the decision to spend a little more money for just the right look or to save some money by buying a cheap suit, always choose the right look. The extra money invested will pay dividends time and time again.

Clothing Tips

The following are some suggestions for most business interview situations. Something else might work, but these tips are pretty standard.

1. Dark suits are best for men, in blue, gray, or perhaps brown (the brown suit was resurrected by President Reagan). Pinstripes are also okay, as long as the stripe is tasteful and doesn't resemble the suit of a mobster. The suit should be conservatively cut and should not look as if you are headed for the disco. The same advice applies to women. A conservative business suit is best for the interview, and the hemline should be at mid-knee or slightly below. A wider variety of colors and shades is fine for women but not for men. Dresses are acceptable as well, but a business suit goes over better.

2. Wear a white shirt with a plain collar—no button-downs or little gold collar pins. Plain collars give a neater appearance, and you won't have to worry about losing the pin or a collar button just before you go in for the interview. The tie should be conservative and the color matched to the suit. The blouse for women should be middle of the road: not too frilly, but also not too severe.

3. Accessories should complement the outfit. Again, remember that you are going for an interview and not out on a date. Don't wear excessive amounts of jewelry, such as a diamond pinky ring or a gold nugget wristwatch band (especially if you are going to work for a bank). The only lapel pin you should wear is something like the American flag or a military service pin. Others, such as those representing fraternal groups, could evoke some of the personal prejudices from the interviewer as discussed in Chapter 4.

4. Shoes should be appropriate for the event. If you are going into a position where you will work with your hands,
wear a substantial pair of work boots. In most other situations men should wear a dark-colored business-type
shoe, such as wing tips, or a plain single toe cap. Be sure
they are well shined and sole dressing is used. Women
should wear a dark, plain, medium-heeled, closed-toe
pump.

Interview Accessories

If you're going for a business interview, you probably think you
need a briefcase, but we recommend a portfolio to carry under
your arm. A briefcase is clumsy to carry and can get in your
way very easily. A portfolio under your arm can be handled much
more adeptly. Empty the case of all items except those that at-
test to your qualifications. Leave out personal items that you
might otherwise carry around in your case, such as your lunch,
correspondence, and the bills you picked up out of your mailbox
that morning. The only items in the case should be extra resumes, licenses, examples of your work, degrees, diplomas, cer-
tificates, transcripts, and a list of your references.

Advance Work

If you've never been to the interview location before, and if you
have the time, go there before the interview and check out any
possible problems with traffic, directions, and parking. (You
might discover in advance that you don't even want the job after
you've evaluated potential commute problems.) This recon-
naissance will also allow you to time your trip properly on the
day of the interview. A friend of ours once had an appointment
in downtown Miami in July. He planned his trip to arrive at the
place about ten minutes before his appointment, but failed to
realize that the closest parking was seven blocks away. He had
to park the car and sprint seven blocks through downtown
Miami in the heat to get there almost on time. With the heat
and humidity, you can imagine how he looked.

Advance Research

Well before the interview, make certain you research the company or organization and, if possible, the interviewers themselves. My toughest interview was for a judicial fellowship at the Supreme Court of the United States. The interview panel consisted of several trial and appellate federal judges, the administrative assistant to the chief justice, the retired chairman of the board of a major steel company, a former dean of Harvard Law School, and several other heavyweights. To prepare, I researched each panel member, committing various biographical data to memory. During the evening before the interview, the nine finalists were invited to dinner with the panel members. At my table sat the administrative assistant to the chief justice, a Mormon who (I had learned) had spent his two-year mission in Argentina. At one of those inevitable lulls in the conversation I turned to him and asked how he enjoyed his stay in Argentina. His mouth dropped open and he asked, "How did you know about my mission to Argentina?" I shot back, "Well, sir, the panel has received a great deal of information about me, so I thought it only fair that I find out something about each panel member." At that point, I firmly believe, I won the fellowship.

You do the same. Visit the company before the interview. Call friends who know something about the company. Get a copy of the annual report. Do a search on CompuServe or other computer database for any recent stories on the company. Do anything you can to find out vital information, and then make certain you reveal this knowledge at some point in the interview. This one trick will work wonders.

Punctuality

You should arrive at the appropriate office at least ten minutes before the appointed time, but not more than fifteen. If you arrive an hour early, as over-achievers tend to do, you will throw the interview schedule off, and it may work against you. Further, if you have to sit around the office for any length of time, they will have a longer period to look at you and consider you an imposition in their day rather than a welcome, timely visitor.

In the Office

If you smoke, leave your cigarettes in the car. Even if the interviewer smokes, you should not. It is impossible to maintain eye contact while you're smoking. Three out of four people are nonsmokers anyway. In fact, you should remove any bulky items from your pocket, such as keys, papers, or other paraphernalia.

When you arrive, you will probably be asked to fill out a long application for employment. Be sure you bring enough information with you to complete this form. Items such as dates, addresses, and names can be hard to remember. Take your time with this form and fill it out completely. Don't write, "see resume" in place of data; if the company had wanted only to see your resume, it would not have asked you to complete the form. Because resumes differ so greatly, most companies like to use an application form. It ensures they get all of the information they need in the format they prefer. If you are prepared and fill out the form completely, you will again be ahead of the other candidates who have not read this book.

Assume everyone who has contact with you at the company on the day of the interview may be asked to evaluate you. If an employment manager is trying to decide between two candidates for a position and can't make up her mind, the first person she will ask for an opinion will be her secretary. You can be sure she is going to give her a candid view of her impressions. Act professional, but not stiff. Be friendly and conversational, but don't talk too much with the office staff. Be careful not to try to get too friendly or personal with them; they may go to lunch with you, but you won't get the job.

Before you're finally ushered in to meet the interviewer, make a last-minute check of your personal appearance. For men, is your tie straight? Are your socks pulled up tight? Are they the same color? Lapel pin right-side up? Shoes clean and shined? Hair combed? Portfolio under the left arm? (Leave the right free for handshakes.)

For women, are your makeup and lipstick okay? Shoes clean and shined? Hosiery okay? Slip showing? Hair neat?

Your Grand Debut

Everything checks out? Okay, go ahead and make your entrance. Walk straight to the interviewer and offer your hand and a pleasant smile. Be careful not to make the handshake too firm (you are not applying to be the stand-in for Arnold Schwarzenegger) or too limp. Grasp the other person's hand completely, not just the fingers for one of those dead fish handshakes. If you are wearing a jacket (suit coat), unbutton it before sitting down, then ensure it hangs properly and is not bunched up and gaping open. (Practice sitting down in front of a mirror. See how you appear from the other side of the desk.) Women should be extra careful about the skirt riding up, and men should be mindful of hairy ankles peeking out over the socks.

Now some philosophy: As I said, the conduct of the interview is the responsibility of the interviewer. A skillful interviewer will control all facets of the conversation and guide you through a logical plan in order to uncover specific items of information. Some questions will be directed at gaining data, and others will be used to determine your thought process.

Usually, you will undergo more than one interview. The first will be conducted by human resources professionals who will totally control the direction of the conversation. That's their job, what they are trained to do, and you have little choice but to go with the flow. Second or subsequent interviews are conducted by people who make hiring decisions, but who have little or no training in interview techniques. If you understand the process, sometimes you can take control of the interview and help to guide the interviewer to the proper conclusion—to hire you.

The Interview

The interviewer will most likely take the following steps with you:

Establish Rapport.   The interviewer's responsibility is to put you at ease, both physically and emotionally. The more relaxed you are, the more you will trust the interviewer and open up to him or her. Skilled interviewers will not put you in front of a desk. They will put the chair beside the desk that so there are no barriers between you, or will not use a desk at all. Initial conversation will be about trivial matters such as the weather, parking, or any subject to get you talking.

Determine Your Qualifications.   The interviewer has to find out as early as possible if you are technically qualified (on the surface) for the job. Time is valuable, and an interviewer can't waste it on unqualified candidates. The determination is made by a review of the application and your resume. This can turn into a simple yes and no session as the interviewer matches your qualifications against the requirements for the position. During this phase, information is gathered to develop questions later on in the conversation. This technique is called blueprinting.

Explain the Company and the Job.   At this point in the interview, the interviewer will try to get you excited about wanting to work for the company. He or she generally will cover job responsibilities and company benefits to interest you even further.

Determine Your Suitability.   The interviewer now has to determine if you are the best candidate. In many cases this is a subjective judgment based upon impressions of your conduct and your ability to handle the questions posed to you. In this part of the interview you will be asked situational questions, which may or may not be directly related to your future duties. The interviewer may even ask some startling questions to get your response. The technique used is to ask open-ended questions (those that require more than a one-word answer) during this phase, rather than close-ended questions (those that only require a simple yes or no).

Conclusion.   At this point it is the interviewer's responsibility to review the major points you covered during the interview and get you out of the office in a timely manner. The interviewer should ensure all of your questions have been answered and will generally let you know what the next step is and when a decision will be made.

As you can see, an interview is a planned and controlled process. As stated, a trained and skilled interviewer will guide you through the steps and will know exactly how to keep you on track. The managers in the second and subsequent interviews may not follow a planned agenda and may even have trouble staying on track themselves. If you understand what is happening, you can take control. The rules for the interview are based on one theory only. If you were called, you probably are qualified for the job. Your task is to show the company you are the best qualified of the candidates who are competing. Here are some suggestions for doing that.

Always Be Positive. Losers dwell on past losses, winners dwell on future successes. Don't worry about where you have been, worry about where you're going. Make sure your accomplishments are related to your capabilities.

Listen, Listen, Listen. Throughout the interview, concentrate to be sure you're really listening to what the interviewer has to say. It looks very bad when you ask a question the interviewer just answered.

State Your Qualifications, Not Your Drawbacks. Tell them what you can do; let them wonder about what you can't do.

Ask Questions. Be sure to ask intelligent, well-thought-out questions that indicate you are trying to find out what you can do for the company. Base any statements on proven experience, not dreams and hopes.

Watch Out for Close-Ended Questions. Be wary of interviewers who ask close-ended questions. They probably don't know what they are doing. If you begin to hear a series of questions that require only a yes or no, the other candidates are probably hearing the same questions. If the interviewer asks three candidates the same question and all he gets are three no answers, he won't be able to distinguish among the three. If all the answers are the same, he can't make an intelligent choice. Your strategy, then, is to turn these close-ended questions into open-ended ones so you can put a few intelligent sentences together. In this way, you will distinguish yourself from the other yes and no candidates.

Stay Focused.   Concentrate on the conversation at hand. Don't get off on extraneous matters that have nothing to do with the job or your qualifications.

Don't Get Personal.   Keep personal issues out of the interview. Never confide in an interviewer no matter how relaxed and comfortable you feel. If you feel the urge to bare your soul, your feelings should tell you the interviewer is very skilled and followed the first step of the interview extremely well.

Rehearse.   Plan some answers to obvious questions. Why did you leave your previous position? Why did you choose your academic major? What are your training and experience going to do for the company?

Maintain Eye Contact.   If you can't look interviewers in the eye, they won't believe your answer. Further, there are no answers written on the ceiling, so if you get in a bind, don't look up for divine guidance. The answer is not on the ceiling. It's in your head.

Pause a Moment.   Take a moment before each answer to consider what you will say. Don't answer the question in a rush, but reflect a moment to get it straight.

Take Notes.   If you plan on taking notes, ask first. Some people are uncomfortable when their words are written down. Do not attempt to record the conversation.

Multiple Interviewers.   If you are interviewed by more than one person, answer all of them equally. Begin with the questioner, let your eyes go to each of the others as you continue your answer, and finally come back to the original questioner. Each of them will then feel you are speaking to him or her alone.

Don't Drink, Don't Smoke. In fact, don't ingest anything at all. Although it is polite to accept a proffered cup of coffee or a soft drink, it is not polite to spill it in your lap. You will be nervous, so don't take the chance. Remember, they are merely trying to establish rapport. Besides, you can't maintain eye contact while drinking or eating.

Likely Open-Ended Questions. What follows are some properly formulated open-ended questions you may hear later. Get used to the format and prepare answers. Keep them down to a couple of sentences, not three paragraphs.

1. In your relationship with your previous supervisor, would you mind giving an example of how you were alike or not alike?
2. How would you define success?
3. Would you demonstrate some methods you would use to cause a marginal employee to rise to his or her full potential?
4. How can a team atmosphere improve your personal effectiveness?
5. If you were a problem, how would you solve yourself?

After the Interview

When the interview concludes, don't linger, but don't run out the door, either. If the interviewers haven't indicated when a decision will be reached, ask them. This will give them the impression that you might have other offers you are considering. When you get back to your car, take out a professional-looking note card (purchased in advance for just this purpose) and write (in longhand with a roller pen or a fountain pen) a brief thank-you note to all the people in the company who interviewed you. The note should say something like the note on the next page.

Thank-you note.

> Dear Ms. Jones:
>
> It was a pleasure to meet you, and I appreciate the oppor-
> tunity to compete for the position of high speed yo-yo
> operator. The job offers a real challenge, and I am very in-
> terested in joining the team. I'll await your decision.
>
> > Sincerely,
> >
> > Joseph D. Ragman

Take the note to the post office and mail it the same day. It is important that the note reach the interviewer the next day. You hope it will hit her desk at the same time she is comparing your resume with other candidates'. You now have the advantage of having at least two documents on her desk with your name on them. It might not help, but it certainly won't hurt.

Facing the interview might make you apprehensive, but there is no reason to fear it. It is your real opportunity to get face to face with your product's potential buyer and bring to bear all of your personal selling skills. If you go into the situation with confidence based on preparation and not on ego, you will come out a winner. Take the time to prepare properly. The interview has been your goal thus far in the job search, so it is your stepping stone to future success. Be positive, be enthusiastic, and rely on your experience in communicating with people.

CHAPTER 12

You Want *How* Much?

Salary Negotiation

SALARY NEGOTIATION BEGINS WITH knowledge. Remember that personal ideas concerning your value to an employer are generally based on desire and not on reality. Otherwise, remember this economic fact of life: You are only worth what your skills are worth in a specific marketplace.

Knowing What You're Worth

An Air Force master sergeant who was leaving the service was discussing salary with a recruiter. He was a communications specialist and had agreed to start work with the company in three weeks. When the recruiter asked him for his salary requirements, he said he had done some research and talked to his friends in industry, and he really had to have compensation somewhere in the neighborhood of $20,000 to $22,000. The recruiter looked him squarely in the eye and said, "I sure am glad to hear that because I was going to offer you thirty-one-five!" In this case, the applicant was paid the $31,500 because the company is extremely reputable and believes in taking care of people. Others, less reputable, would have hired him at the lower amount. Six months later, when he found he had got a raw deal and quit, they could probably have found another person selling himself short. You can't afford to make that kind of mistake. This person obviously had not prepared for the negotiation and could easily have been burned.

Salary negotiation should be based upon the good principles of sales we have been following throughout the job search. You would not try to buy or sell an automobile unless you had first checked the NADA *Blue Book* to determine the value of the vehicle. Otherwise you would never know if you were getting (or paying) the true value.

In Chapter 9 we reviewed some ideas and sources to check out your salary expectations, and now is the time to put that information to work. Remember, this is a buy-sell situation. You are trying to get the highest pay for your services, and the employer is trying to get your services as economically as possible.

The Power of the Purse

As you talk with future employers, you will find it interesting that, in many cases, the individual who has the hiring authority (manager, director, supervisor, or foreman) seldom has the authority to determine your compensation level. Compensation is controlled by the human resources department because in many companies they own the salary budget. Their mission is to keep the cost per hire low and to keep all other compensation programs within reasonable limits. Many companies also have strict policies on starting salary, but others are flexible. Because you won't know which you are dealing with, you will need a strategy to ensure you get the best possible deal.

Learning to Bump

Compensation programs are structured in most companies to place salary within a range. That means as long as you remain in a certain position, you will make no less than the minimum for that position and no more than the maximum. The ranges are usually divided into steps, sometimes called quartiles or quintiles, to allow for normal advancement within the position. You may or may not know the range for the position you are seeking. You should assume any offers will be at the low end of the range. Your tactic will be to bump the offer to see if it can be raised by 10 percent.

After a successful interview you will probably be called back to meet with the human resources people again. At that time the administrative formalities will be taken care of, and salary will be decided upon. This is where you can negotiate. When the offer comes, you should immediately evaluate it to determine if it is fair. Considerations should include benefits, advancement potential, and interest in the position. You should review information gained in your research and confirmed by your visits to the state employment service and private employment agencies.

Learning to Say No

If the offer is not fair, reject it immediately. State your reasons and your sources of information by saying, "That's not really a reasonable offer. I have done quite a bit of research and talked to the state employment service, and I know widget designers make at least _____ in this market." The figure you quote should be the most current information you have and include a 10 percent error factor. For example, if your research indicates widget designers make $20,000 in that marketplace, you should quote $22,000. Then, you should sit back and await the response to determine if you want to negotiate further or just decline the job.

If the offer is a fair one and you feel comfortable with it, then bump it by 10 percent. "Mr. Jones, that's really a fair offer, but I was thinking more along the lines of $ _____ ." Now don't go crazy and ask for 50 percent, and don't forget to consider the benefits. Perhaps a little bit less might be fair for a great benefits package and a little bit more for a weak package, but always ask for 10 percent. In many cases you will find the recruiter was holding some back to sweeten the deal for your services. After all, companies are in competition for your services and might pay just a little bit extra to get you. If you don't ask, you will never know.

Learning to Say Yes

If the recruiter indicates they are restricted by company policy and must start everyone at the bottom end of the scale, then you merely accept the offer by saying, "Okay, I'll take the job. When may I expect a compensation review?" Generally speaking, with the review you either get a raise or you get fired. Anyway, nothing ventured, nothing gained.

Determining Income

If you are asked to provide your salary requirements or expectations, consider the median income for the skill or position in that marketplace and then add 10 percent. Again, be prepared to cite your sources. If you state your case with enough confidence, the recruiter might even feel his wage and salary information is out of date and check to see when the last review was done. This could also work in your favor.

If you decide to think the offer over because of pending interviews with other employers, be sure to ask the interviewer how long the offer is good for. Don't take the chance of waiting too long and losing the opportunity to another candidate.

Benefits

A solid package of benefits can make a weak salary offer look much more inviting. Benefits are a major portion of your total compensation package and can cost a company as much as 20 to 30 percent above your cash salary, including Social Security contributions and unemployment insurance. The following are some of the benefits offered by various companies in today's workplace.

Medical Care. Most companies offer some form of medical insurance. The best will cover you and your family at no cost to you, but many companies are now dropping the family coverage, because of cost. In those cases, you can usually cover your family for an additional premium deducted from your paycheck. Most will include some form of deductible you will have to pay.

Dental Care. This is one benefit everyone needs. Again, most companies offer this benefit to you and might cover your family for a fee, and you probably will have to pay deductibles.

Short- or Long-Term Disability. This is a plan offered by some companies to continue a portion of your pay for varying periods if you are disabled. This is a great benefit to have if something unforeseen happens and you can't work, because you'll know your family will have some income.

Life Insurance. Many companies automatically include life insurance in their benefit packages. The face value of the policy is generally linked to your annual income level.

Parking. Free parking can be a real benefit if you are employed in a center city somewhere. Monthly parking can cost you fifty dollars or more a month, and many companies that don't own their own lots will reimburse employees for parking expenses.

401K Plan. 401Ks are savings plans that allow you to save up to 6 percent of your gross salary with the interest being tax deferred. In these plans the company participates and matches your contribution by fifty cents or more for each dollar you save. Vesting will occur after a period of years, and most plans will allow you to borrow against your savings. After you are vested, you can withdraw the money upon leaving the company or retiring. Only then will you incur any tax liability.

Vacation. For executives, the time might be negotiable. Most companies have plans that increase your vacation time as you remain in the organization for several years.

Paid Holidays. You can generally expect to get approximately eight to ten paid holidays each year, unless you are in the retail trade. Obviously, most stores are open during most holidays and weekends. If you go to work for a company that requires weekend work, you can probably negotiate which weekdays you are given off.

Overtime. Although this is not exactly a benefit, it would be nice to know the company's overtime policy. How much overtime is paid, how often it can be expected, and whether it is voluntary or mandatory are good questions to ask.

Automobile. Some sales and executive positions as well as some service industries provide you with a vehicle. This can be a valuable asset if you commute. The savings in gas, insurance, and monthly payments can be substantial. It's important to know if the car can be used for personal business.

Auto Allowance. An allowance in lieu of a vehicle can be a great asset as well. If the amount is fair, it can save you a lot of money and provide some tax advantages as well. You will have to keep accurate records, but it is a solid benefit.

Expenses. If you are required to travel, you will want to learn the rules for expenses. Does the employer reimburse all expenses on the road, or only a portion? Are there limits on where you can stay and eat? Answers to these questions will give you some real insights into corporate policy as it regards people.

Other Compensation

There are several forms of compensation other than a straight salary. Generally, salaried positions offer the most complete package of benefits because you are formally employed by the company. There are other positions, usually in sales or consulting, where you are an agent or are merely providing service to the company. Obviously, if you are self-employed, you can decide what benefits you want to provide for yourself.

Sales people are motivated by money. Consequently, they want to get paid for what they do. Most sales people who work on commission do so because they want to be the masters of their own destinies. If they want a raise, they just work a little harder. If they want time off, they just take it. The amount of money to be made is limited only by desire and need.

Within sales there are several methods of payment. First is straight commission with no salary. These types of positions generally pay the highest percentages of commission and generally require the individual to purchase his own benefits. Next is the draw, which allows the sales person to receive a specified amount monthly (or weekly), and any sales commissions are deducted from this amount. Benefits might or might not be included. If sales exceed the draw, the higher amount is paid. Finally, there is salary plus commission. In this system, the sales person receives a salary and benefits, and then receives a commission on top of the salary when each sale is completed.

Consultants are paid a negotiated amount to provide a specified service to an organization. This is generally a fixed amount and is paid in either a lump sum or installments over the life of the contract. Benefits are not included because the consultant is really independent. People who work for a consulting firm are usually salaried employees of that company, and compensation would be paid as it would for any other company with accompanying benefits.

If you take a position where you are paid a commission or a consulting fee, you will be responsible for paying not only your own benefits but also your own taxes and Social Security. Social Security will also require you to pay the amount your employer would normally contribute. Be sure to talk to a tax accountant or an attorney to get some help in effectively evaluating those types of compensation packages.

Knowledge Is Power

Remember, knowledge is the key. You can do very well in negotiating and evaluating compensation offers. All you need to do is to gather some information. So check out all of the options, and determine what's right for you. You will then feel much more confident in determining and obtaining a fair wage for your services. Don't just take what someone is going to offer. Ask the right questions and be ready to tell them what you're worth.

CHAPTER 13

P.S.

Your Job

NOW YOU CAN ANSWER no to that loaded question, does your resume wear blue jeans? But your success in following the guidelines in this book raises another intriguing question, can you now live up to your resume? Of course you can, you say. After all, you are the person who has had the experiences detailed on the resume. But there's more to the question than this. Thanks to the steps you've followed here, your resume is more than a list of experiences. It's an advertising piece which conveys to employers that you have not only the experience but also the qualities they're looking for. The resume is designed to show those qualities. So the way to live up to your resume is to demonstrate them.

Thus, following our checklist of qualities in Chapter 1, you will communicate, conduct business intelligently, exercise self-confidence, accept responsibility, take the initiative, lead, channel energy into your work, use your imagination, be flexible, get along with others, know yourself, handle conflict, achieve goals, compete in a healthy way, exercise and develop your skills, and follow your inner sense of direction. Simple, right? Not necessarily the things you learned in kindergarten, all of them, but close.

So after writing this glowing document about yourself, it's time to give your own performance a careful look. It's time to set some standards, standards living up to the picture you've painted of yourself. It's time to realize the kind of service you would expect if you were hiring you. You would want a high level of excellence. Begin early in your career to deliver that level of performance, and success will always come your way. Good luck.

Appendix

List of Action Verbs

accelerated	assisted	changed	convinced
accomplished	assumed	checked	coordinated
accounted for	assured	chopped	copied
achieved	attended	chose	corrected
acquired	authored	classified	counseled
added	authorized	cleared up	counted
adjusted	awarded	closed	crafted
administered	began	combined	created
advised	bolstered	communicated	criticized
aided	boosted	compared	dealt
alphabetized	bought	completed	debated
analyzed	briefed	composed	decided
anticipated	brought	conceived	defined
applied	budgeted	concluded	delegated
appointed	built	conditioned	delivered
appraised	calculated	conducted	demonstrated
arbitrated	catalogued	constructed	designed
argued	caught	continued	determined
arranged	caused	contracted	developed
assessed	chaired	controlled	devised

digested	grabbed	mapped out	purchased
diminished	graded	maximized	put
directed	greeted	met	qualified
discovered	grossed	modified	quickened
drafted	guided	monitored	ran
dramatized	handled	motivated	rated
drew up	hastened	moved	realized
dropped	heightened	named	received
earned	helped	neatened	recognized
edited	highlighted	negotiated	recommended
educated	hiked	netted	reduced
elected	housed	observed	renovated
employed	hunted	opened	reported
encouraged	identified	operated	rescued
enjoyed	implemented	ordered	researched
enlarged	improved	organized	resulted in
enlisted	included	overcame	returned
ensured	incorporated	oversaw	revealed
entered	increased	paid	reviewed
established	indicated	painted	revised
estimated	initiated	participated	said
evaluated	innovated	perceived	saved
excelled	inspected	performed	saw
executed	instructed	persuaded	scouted
exercised	insured	pioneered	screened
expanded	interpreted	placed	scrutinized
expedited	interviewed	planned	selected
explained	introduced	played	sent
explored	investigated	policed	served
familiarized	joined	prepared	set
filed	kept	presented	shipped
financed	labored	prevailed	shored up
forecast	launched	processed	showed
foresaw	lectured	produced	sifted
formulated	led	profited	simplified
forwarded	licensed	programmed	smoothed
fostered	located	prohibited	solved
found	looked	projected	sought
gained	made	promoted	spearheaded
gathered	maintained	proofed	specified
gave	managed	proved	spoke

started
stated
stopped
straightened
streamlined
strengthened
stripped
studied
submitted
suggested
summarized

supervised
supported
surmounted
surveyed
targeted
taught
tested
tightened
took
took over
totaled

toured
tracked
trained
transferred
transformed
translated
traveled
treated
tutored
typed
uncovered

unearthed
unfurled
updated
upped
welcomed
won
worked
wrote

List of Adjectives and Adverbs

academic (ally)
accurate (ly)
active (ly)
adventurous (ly)
aggressive (ly)
alert (ly)
ambitious (ly)
analytical (ly)
artistic (ally)
assertive (ly)
attractive (ly)
bold (ly)
broad-minded (ly)
businesslike
calm (ly)
capable (ably)
careful (ly)
cautious (ly)
challenging
cheerful (ly)
clever (ly)
competent (ly)
competitive (ly)
confident (ly)

conscientious (ly)
conservative (ly)
considerate (ly)
consistent (ly)
cooperative (ly)
courageous (ly)
creative (ly)
curious (ly)
deliberate (ly)
determined (ly)
dignified
discreet (ly)
dominant (ly)
eager (ly)
easygoing
efficient (ly)
energetic (ally)
enormous (ly)
fair-minded (ly)
farsighted
firm (ly)
flexible (ibly)
forceful (ly)
formal (ly)
frank (ly)

friendly
generous (ly)
good-natured (ly)
healthy
helpful (ly)
high (ly)
honest (ly)
huge (ly)
humorous (ly)
imaginative (ly)
imposing (ly)
independent (ly)
individualistic
industrious (ly)
informal (ly)
intellectual (ly)
intelligent (ly)
inventive (ly)
kind (ly)
large (ly)
leisurely
liberal (ly)
likable (ably)
logical (ly)
loyal (ly)

mammoth
mature (ly)
methodical (ly)
meticulous (ly)
mild (ly)
moderate (ly)
modest (ly)
motivated
natural (ly)
obliging (ly)
opportunistic (ally)
optimistic (ally)
organized
original (ly)
outgoing
painstaking (ly)
patient (ly)
persevering
pleasant (ly)
poised
polite (ly)
practical (ly)
precise (ly)
progressive (ly)
prudent (ly)

purposeful (ly)
quick (ly)
quiet (ly)
rational (ly)
realistic (ally)
reflective (ly)
relaxed
reliable (ably)
reserved (ly)
resourceful (ly)
responsible
  (ibly)
robust (ly)

self-confident
  (ly)
self-controlled
sensible (ibly)
sensitive (ly)
serious (ly)
significant (ly)
sincere (ly)
sociable (ably)
spontaneous (ly)
stable
steady (ily)
strong (ly)

strong-minded
  (ly)
successful (ly)
supportive
tactful (ly)
teachable
tenacious (ly)
thorough (ly)
thoughtful (ly)
tolerant (ly)
tough
trustworthy
unaffected (ly)

understanding
  (ly)
unexcitable
  (ably)
uninhibited (ly)
verbal (ly)
versatile
warm (ly)
wise (ly)
witty (ily)
zany (ily)

Index

Abbreviation, writing style, 117–119
Accomplishments
  education heading, 81
  portraying on resume, 25–30
Acronym, abbreviation, 118–119
Activities, 92–94
  college students, 94
  high school students, 94
  self-assessment, 33
Address
  in caption, 59–61
  current, 60–61
  graphics of caption, 126–128
  home, 60–61
  list, compiling, 167
  mail campaign, 186
  office, 60–61
  permanent, 60–61
  on resume, 100
  school, 60–61
Adjectives
  list of, 235–236
  use of, 121
Adverbs
  list of, 235–236
  use of, 121
Advertisement, resume, 39
Age, on resume, 98, 101
Agencies. See Employment agencies

Alumni, college placement office,
    199–200
American Almanac of Jobs and
    Salaries, 170
Americans With Disabilities Act, 101
Annual Salary Survey for College
    Graduates, 170
Answering machine, use of, 100
Application form, interview, 216
Asterisk, use of, 138–139
Athletics, 94–95
  high school students, 90–91
  traits employers seek, 16
Attributes
  portraying on resume, 25–30
  traits employers seek, 5–19
Automobile, salary negotiation, 228
Availability, date of, 101
Awards, 78–80
  self-assessment, 33
  subheading of education, 74

Babysitting, high school students,
    90–91
Band, high school students, 90–91
BASIC, 97
Benefits
  salary negotiation, 226–228
  self-marketing, 2–3

Big city, questions in self-assessment, 37–38
Bold
  graphics of emphasis, 136–137
  word processing, 147
Boy Scouts, high school students, 90–91
Briefcase, interview, 214
Bullet, use of, 138–139
Business Periodicals Index, 170

Campus, recruiting, 204–206
Capitalization
  graphics of emphasis, 136–137
  writing style, 117
Caption, 59–61
  graphics, 126–129
  two addresses, 60–61, 127–128
Career Guide, 209
Career objective. *See* Objective
Career planning. *See* Placement office
Centered heading, sample, 131
Children
  information on resume, 99–100
  questions in self-assessment, 37–38
Chronological resume, 51–53
  sample headings, 68–69
Citizenship, 98
Classified advertisement
  letter responding to, 181–185
  market research, 170–171
  National Business Employment Weekly, 174
  need for resume, 40
Clothing
  importance of images, 124
  interviews, 212–214
Clubs, information on resume, 99
COBOL, 97
College, incomplete education, 76
College Placement Council, employer survey, 4–19
College placement office. *See* Placement office
College students
  activities, 94
  experience on resume, 26–27
  objective, 61–62
  placement office, 198–209
  sample personal profile, 65
  self-assessment, 31–32
  typical summer job, 83–84
Color, paper, 150–151
Combat boots, companion book, 96

Combination resume, 51, 56–57
Commemorative stamp, cover letter, 190
Commission, salary negotiation, 229
Communication skills
  portraying, 73
  traits employers seek, 5–6
Community service, 95
  self-assessment, 33
Competitive edge, focus of job search, 2–3
Competitiveness, traits employers seek, 15–16
Computer languages, 97
Content, resume, 71–102
Continuing education, portraying, 76–77
Copies, of resume, 149–150
Cotton, paper type, 150–151
Counseling. *See* Placement office
Cover letters, 176–189
  classified advertisement, 181–185
  mass mailing, 185–187
  paper type, 151
  personalizing, 187–189
Creativity, traits employers seek, 11
Creed, excluded from resume, 98
Date, 109–112
  defined, 67
  degree, 110
  employment, 110
Date of birth, caption creativity, 128
Dean's List, honors on resume, 79–80
Degree, date of, 110
Dental care, salary negotiation, 227
Desktop publishing, production of resume, 147–148
Dingbat, graphic device, 139
Direction
  portraying, 73
  traits employers seek, 18–19
Directory of Directories, 169
Directory of Employment Resources, 169–170
Directory of Executive Recruiters, headhunters, 195
Directory of Information Services, 169
Disability, salary negotiation, 227
Does Your Resume Wear Combat Boots?, 96
Dollars, using numbers, 121–122
Dot matrix printer, production of resume, 147

Dress for Success
  importance of images, 123
  interview suit, 212
Duns Marketing Service Million-Dollar Directory, 169

Education, 72–78
  creating lead, 106–107
  examples of heading, 77–78
  placement on resume, 103
  self-assessment, 31–32
Emerson's Directory of Leading U.S. Accounting Firms, 169
Employment, 80–92
  accomplishments, 81
  contents of entry, 80
  creating lead, 107–108
  date of, 110
  manipulating heading, 104
  multiple jobs, 85–86
  multiple positions, 84–85
  self-assessment, 32–33
Employment advertisement. *See* Classified advertisement
Employment agencies, 194–197
Employment manager, 44–46
Energy level, traits employers seek, 10
Entry
  defined, 67
  margin for, 129, 132
Envelopes, cover letters, 189–190
Ethnic origin, excluded from resume, 98
Expenses, salary negotiation, 228
Experts, varying opinions, 50–51
Externships, college placement office, 207–208
Eye contact, interview, 220

False information, excluded from resume, 20
Features, self-marketing, 2–3
Fee, employment agencies, 196, 197
First person pronoun, writing, 114–115
Flexibility, traits employers seek, 11–12
Font, production of resume, 147
Footnote, resume technique, 105–106
Foreign languages, 96–97
Foreign travel, 95–96
Format, 123–143
  samples, 156–163
  word processing, 147
FORTRAN, 97

Fortune's Directory of U.S. Corporations, 169
401K Plan, salary negotiation, 227
Functional resume, 51, 53–56
  sample headings, 69–70
Functional subheadings
  people over 30, 87–89
  samples, 68, 70, 88–89
Functional subheading resume, 51, 57–58

Girl Scouts, high school students, 90–91
Goal achievement, traits employers seek, 15
Grade point average
  problems with, 74–75
  self-assessment, 32
  traits employers seek, 6–7
Grammatical mistakes, 115–119
Graphics of emphasis, 136–139
  mistakes, 139–142
Graphics of positioning, 126–136
GRE scores
  portraying, 75
  self-assessment, 32

Headhunters, use of, 196
Heading
  centered, 129, 131
  chronological resume examples, 68–69
  defined, 67
  functional, 53–56
  functional, examples, 69–70
  graphic mistake, 140
  graphics of positioning, 129–133
  left margin, 129–130
  long, 132–133
  modifying, 69
  samples for homemakers, 90
Health, on resume, 101
Height, information on resume, 99
Hidden job market, 173–174, 175–176
High school, including on resume, 75–76
High school students
  activities, 94
  employment, 90–91
  objective, 61–62
  sample personal profile, 65
  self-assessment, 32
Holidays, salary negotiation, 228

Homemakers
employment, 89–90
experience on resume, 27–28
sample personal profile, 65
self-assessment, 32
Honesty, 78–80
self-assessment, 33
subheading of education, 74
traits employers seek, 19–20
Horizontal spacing, graphics of emphasis, 136, 138
Human resource manager, 44–46

Imagination, traits employers seek, 8
Industry, objective, 62
Initiative, traits employers seek, 9
Integrity, traits employers seek, 20
Intelligence
portraying, 73
traits employers seek, 5–7
Interests, 97–98
Internships, college placement office, 207–208
Interpersonal skills, traits employers seek, 12–13
Interviews, 211–222
campus recruiting, 204–206
close-ended questions, 218
clothing, 212–214
eye contact, 220
function of resume, 43
open-ended questions, 218
prospecting for, 165–176
punctuality, 215
research, 215
thank-you letter, 221–222
Italics, graphics of emphasis, 136–137

Job, self-assessment, 35–37
Job fairs, college placement office, 204
Job listings, college placement office, 201

Languages, 96–97
Laser printer
copies of resume, 149
cover letters, 189–190
production of resume, 147
Lead, 106–109
defined, 67
graphic mistake, 140
Leadership, traits employers seek, 9–10
Left-margin heading, sample, 131
Length, number of pages, 71

Letters of recommendation, college placement office, 203–204
Liberal arts, vocational skills, 17–18
Library
college placement office, 201–202
prospecting for interviews, 166–167
Life insurance, salary negotiation, 227
Listening skills, traits employers seek, 5–6
Listing, defined, 113–114
Location
objective, 62
self-assessment, 35–37
LSAT scores
portraying, 75
self-assessment, 32

MacWrite, production of resume, 147
Managers
experience on resume, 28–30
sample personal profile, 65
self-assessment, 32
Margin
left-hand, 126
multiple, 132, 134–135
right justified, 147
Marital status, information on resume, 99–100
Marketing, job search, 2–3
Mass mailing, 185–187
need for resume, 40
MCAT scores, portraying, 75
Medical care, salary negotiation, 227
Microsoft Word, production of resume, 147
Military service, 96
Money, self-assessment, 35–37
Multiple objectives, 64–65
Municipal and Government Manuals, 170

Name
in caption, 59–61
graphics of caption, 126–128
on resume, 100
National Business Employment Weekly, 171
classified advertisements, 174
objective, 65
National Job Bank, 169
National League of Cities Directory, 169
Networking, need for resume, 40
Newsletter, college placement office, 200

Newspaper, market research, 173–174
Nickname, excluded in caption, 59–60
Nonparallel construction, grammatical
mistake, 116
Nouns, weak writing style, 119–120
Numbers, use of, 121–122

Objective, 61–67
multiple, 64–65
Occupational Outlook Handbook,
208–209
Odds, in job search, 46–47
Overtime, salary negotiation, 228

PageMaker, production of resume, 147
Paper, resume, 150–151
Parking, salary negotiation, 227
Pascal, 97
Passive voice, writing style, 115
Past tense, writing style, 116
Pay. *See* Salary
Period, use of, 113–114
Periodicals, prospecting for interviews,
167
Personal, information on resume, 98
Personal lead, letter responding to,
185
Personal profile, substitute for objec-
tive, 65
Photocopy, copies of resume, 149
Photographs
no-picture rule, 99
use of, 41
Place of birth, caption creativity, 128
on resume, 100
Placement office, 198–209
library, 166–167
Portfolio, interview, 214
Position
description of, 80–81
lead, 108–109
objective, 62
Positive attitude, traits employers seek,
13
Positive information, included, 71
Post Office, abbreviation of states,
117–119
Present tense, writing style, 116
Product, person as, 1–2
Production of resume, 48–50, 145–152
Professional objective. *See* Objective
Professional resume service, 48–50
pros and cons, 151–152
Pronoun, first person, 114–115

Prospecting
interviews, 165–176
numbers game, 191–192
Public speaking, traits employers seek,
5–6
Publications, 97
Punctuality, interview, 215
Punctuation
graphics of emphasis, 136, 138–139
writing style, 113–114

Quark XPress, production of resume,
147
Questions
close-ended, 218
open-ended, 218, 221
self-assessment, 37–38

Race, excluded from resume, 98
Rand McNally's Commercial Atlas,
170
Reason for leaving, excluding, 82–83
Recruiting, college placement office,
204–206
References, 102–103, 105
self-assessment, 34–35
Refusing salary offer, 225–226
Research
interview, 215
salary negotiation, 229–230
Response rate, mass mailing, 185–187
Responsibility, traits employers seek,
8–9
Resume
advertisement, 39
choice of type, 59
college placement office, 202
content, 71–102
defined, 40–41
footnote, 105–106
need for, 40
paper, 150–151
production of, 145–152
professional writer, 48–50
structure, 59–70
types, 51–58
typical blue jeans resume, 42
word "resume" at top, 60

Salary, 223–230
accepting offer, 225–226
benefits, 226–228
bumping offer, 224–225
excluding, 81

Salary (*continued*)
 including on resume, 82
 questions in self-assessment, 37–38
 refusing offer, 225–226
 researching the market, 168
Salary negotiation, research, 229–230
Sales piece, need for resume, 40
Salespersons, experience on resume,
 28–30
SAT scores
 portraying, 75
 self-assessment, 32
Search firm. *See* Employment agencies
Security clearance, on resume, 100
Self-assessment, 31–35
Self-confidence, traits employers seek,
 7–8
Self-knowledge, traits employers seek,
 13–14
Self-marketing, experience on resume,
 25–30
Seminars, by author, 87
Sentence, writing style, 114–115
Sequencing information, 103–106
Smoking
 information on resume, 99
 interview, 216
Social security number, excluded, 100
Specialty, questions in self-assessment,
 37–38
Speed, traits employers seek, 19–20
*Standard and Poor's Corporate
 Records*, 170
States, abbreviation of, 118
Stress, questions in self-assessment,
 37–38
Stress management, traits employers
 seek, 14
Subheading
 inventing, 104
 samples, 70, 88–89
 type of resume, 87–89
Summer jobs
 college placement office, 207–208
 describing, 83–84

Telephone, follow-up, 190–191
Telephone number
 in caption, 59–61
 on resume, 100
Tense. *See* Verbs

Test scores, portraying, 75
Testing, college placement office,
 202–203
Thank-you letter, interview, 221–222
Thirty-second scan rule, 43–44
Trade journals, prospecting for inter-
 views, 167
Transmittal letters. *See* Cover letters
Travel, 95–96
Typesetting, production of resume, 146
Typing, production of resume, 146

Underlining
 graphics of emphasis, 136–137
 mistakes, 140

Vacation, salary negotiation, 227
Valedictorian, honors on resume, 79–80
Ventura, production of resume, 147
Verbs
 list of, 233–235
 strong writing style, 119–120
 tense, 116
Vertical spacing, graphics of emphasis,
 136, 138
Vocational skills
 portraying, 73
 traits employers seek, 17–18

Wall Street Journal, 65, 171
*Ward's Directory of Largest U.S.
 Corporations*, 169
*Ward's Directory of Private U.S.
 Corporations*, 169
Weight, information on resume, 99
What a Great Idea!, creativity, 11
Where to Find Business Information,
 170
Word processing
 bold, 147
 format, 147
 personalizing cover letters, 187–189
 production of resume, 147–148
WordPerfect, production of resume, 147
WordStar, production of resume, 147
Workshops, college placement office, 203
Writing, 113–122
 ability, traits employers seek, 5–6
 first person pronoun, 114–115
 professional service, 151–152
 punctuation, 113–114

About the Authors

C. Edward Good

C. EDWARD GOOD RECEIVED his law degree in 1971 from the University of Virginia School of Law. In 1975, he accepted an appointment to serve as director of writing at the law school, a position he held until 1980, when he resigned his faculty position and began a series of businesses. One of those businesses, Word Store, a word processing service in Charlottesville, Virginia, developed a broad array of career-search services for students and professionals. As president of the company, Ed began to use his knowledge of effective writing and to apply it to the field of resume and cover-letter writing. He offered a personal service of resume writing and wrote the resumes of more than 2,000 job seekers from 1980 to 1989, when he sold Word Store to Lisa Miller, a University of Virginia graduate and former employee of Word Store.

Ed currently serves as president of LEL Enterprises, a publishing and educational services firm in Charlottesville. He consults with the nation's largest law firms and federal agencies, developing and conducting training programs in powerful writing for lawyers, scientists, engineers, managers, and other professionals.

Ed is the author of several books, including *Mightier than the Sword—Powerful Writing in Class and on the Job* (LEL Enterprises, 1988), and the ghostwriter of the book on creativity by Charles Chic Thompson, *What A Great Idea!* (HarperCollins, 1992).

William G. Fitzpatrick

COMMAND SGT. MAJ. WILLIAM G. FITZPATRICK served in the United States Army for twenty-four years before retiring. He entered the service from the state of Maryland and spent almost seven years in various infantry troop and staff assignments, both in training and actual combat situations. Serving with tactical units in Europe, Korea, Vietnam, and the continental United States earned him, among other military decorations, the Combat Infantryman's Badge, the Legion of Merit, and the Purple Heart.

In 1967, Bill joined the Army Recruiting Command as a field recruiter in Salem, Massachusetts. During the next seventeen years, he gained a wealth of personnel experience, holding every production position within the recruiting command and ultimately reaching the position of command sergeant major of all recruiting activities in the fourteen southwestern states.

Since retiring in late 1984, Bill has traveled throughout the country and abroad as the career transition expert for the Non Commissioned Officers Association (NCOA). He has personally developed a highly regarded series of job seekers workshops designed to assist separating and retiring military personnel planning to enter the civilian job market. These workshops focus on all aspects of the job search and are conducted on major military installations throughout the world.